Twin Flames

Discover How to Find Your Sacred Spiritual Partner, Experience Unconditional Love, Achieve Self-Realization and Live Out Your Soul's Purpose

By Sandra Lopez

© Copyright 2019 - All rights reserved.

Legal Notice:

This book is copyright protected. This book is only for personal use. You cannot amend, distribute, sell, use, quote or paraphrase any part, or the content within this book, without the consent of the author or publisher.

Under no circumstances will any blame or legal responsibility be held against the publisher, or author, for any damage, reparation, or monetary loss, direct or indirect, due to the information contained within this book, including, but not limited to, errors, omissions, or inaccuracies.

Disclaimer Notice:

Please note the information contained within this book is for educational and entertainment purposes only. All effort has been executed to present accurate, up to date, and reliable, complete information. No warranties of any kind are declared or implied. Readers acknowledge that the author is not engaging in the rendering of legal, financial, medical or professional advice. The content within this book has been derived from various sources. Please consult a licensed professional before attempting any techniques outlined in this book.

Table of Contents

Preface 1

Part I: What is a twin flame?

Chapter 1: Twin flames explained 7

Chapter 2: The difference between soulmates and twin flames 19

Chapter 3: A twin flame for everyone 30

Chapter 4: Twin flames are meant to be lovers 42

Part II: Making it easier to find your twin flame

Chapter 5: Getting yourself ready for a reunion 53

Chapter 6: Identifying emotional blockages 69

Chapter 7: Dealing with emotional blockage 84

Chapter 8: Breaking free of those blockages 101

Chapter 9: Attachment in your life is holding you back 116

Chapter 10: Letting go of attachment 132

Part III: Recognizing and living your twin flame

Chapter 11: Recognizing a true twin flame encounter 147

Chapter 12: Identifying a false flame encounter 161

Chapter 13: 18 signs you have met your twin flame 174

Chapter 14: The next steps after meeting your twin flame 187

Chapter 15: The 8 stages of a twin flame relationship 201

Conclusion 212

Preface

Thank you for purchasing this book. Great care was taken to ensure that it delivers the content you expect it to. Since you are very much interested in gaining a deeper and more profound understanding about yourself and those around you, the universe has drawn you to this volume.

Your desire to learn more about yourself has brought you to this point.

If you are just now beginning your journey to self-discovery and self-realization, then welcome. You will find some bumps along the way, but there is nothing about this journey that you will regret. Often, the route can be bumpy but getting to your destination is well worth the wait.

If you have already started down this path, then this book is another step toward that ultimate goal: discovering who you are, what you stand for and how you can change the world around. Please remember that it doesn't necessarily take brave and heroic acts to change the world. Sure, heroes are admired for the great deeds, but heroes don't need to save the world from annihilation.

Heroes save the world one day at a time, one deed at a time.

As you being to discover who you are, one of the most important topics that always arises is: am I meant to be alone?

Everyone ponders this question, one way or another.

In fact, it is perfectly normal for humans to question their existence. Moreover, it is perfectly common to question the circumstances you find yourself in.

For example, you might question why you are alone, why you have lost loved ones, why you have had things go wrong in your life. It is also perfectly normal to feel joy from the good things in life. There is no need to feel guilty because you have had wonderful experiences in life while others haven't.

We aren't all meant to live through the same experience. Otherwise, we would all be robots. If we were all meant to learn the same things, go through the same experiences, at the same time, then there would be no diversity in this world.

When we incarnate into this world, we must go through a series of experiences which will teach us valuable lessons. In a way, life on this Earth is nothing more than a giant school. We must go through various lessons, pass several tests and earn many levels before we can move on to the next step.

Along the way, we have many teachers. These teachers come in all shapes and sizes. Many times, the people that we least expect are the ones that provide us with some of the most important lessons in our lives.

These teachers play many different roles over the course of our lives. In many cases, they come and then they go. Often, it is hard to say good-bye to these wonderful people, but they must go. In a way, we outgrow them. In other ways, they fulfill a purpose in our lives. So, they must go on and serve others. Even if they are terrible people who have done us wrong, their actions teach us a lesson.

As such, it is up to you to distill the lessons that you needed to learn from them.

Sure, life is very easy when everything is going right, but what about when things are not going right? What about all those times when we feel like there is nothing to live for?

That's why this book is for you: the one who questions life, question why we are here, and most importantly, why the people that come into our lives do so.

If you pay close attention to the people that have come and gone in your life, you will be able to see how many people you influenced, whether you realize it, or not. These people were drawn to you for a reason. You helped them achieve something important. And then, when your role was fulfilled, life sort of left you drifting apart.

Now, we are talking about friends, family and lovers. Every person in your life, even a grumpy bank clerk that made life impossible for you, has something to teach you. And, you have something to give back to the world.

Whatever your reality has been up now, you can take it as a lesson learned. You can vow to make something wonderful and useful of your life from now on.

Thus, this book is centered upon finding your twin flame. We will explore what a twin flame is, if it is the same as your soulmate, and if you have already found this magical person.

In a world filled with distractions, it is easy to overlook that marvelous person. In fact, you might be thinking about them right now, as we speak. You might have their face right, dead center in your mind's eye. Perhaps you are now reaching for your phone tempted to contact them.

Or, you might be drawing a blank, wondering if you will ever meet that someone.

If you have that yearning, that longing, that empty spot in the middle of your chest, it is because that someone might be out there searching for you, too.

But this subliminal encounter isn't quite like the movies. It isn't roses and champagne after years of loneliness and grief. You need to become the right person for your twin flame. You can't expect to get the best out of your twin flame if you aren't at your best.

In fact, there might be aspects of you that might be holding you back. As such, the first part in this book is dedicated to identifying who that magical someone is; what a twin flame is and how you can have a clear idea of who that someone might be.

Then, the second part in this book is dedicated to letting you working on your own, personal development so that, when you meet your twin flame, you will be the best version of yourself. You will be able to capture that spark, and rather than run away from them, you will be the rock that they need in their lives.

The third section in this book is devoted to understanding what the twin flame relationship dynamic is. We will uncover the amazing aspects to that relationship. Also, we will look at the obstacles that you might have to face as a result of this relationship. Please bear in mind that everything doesn't always come up roses when you are with your beloved flame.

When you gain a deeper understanding of the relationship dynamic between flames, you will realize why things often happen the way they do. This will give you a sense of peace, but also, it will give you food for thought. So, you will realize what areas of your relationship you need to work on in order to make it work eventually.

Finally, the conclusion in this book is all about taking the first steps that you need in order to be ready for your twin flame. If you believe you already know this person, then improving yourself will help you get over the hurdles you need in order to become the person they need you to be.

If you haven't, then improving yourself will help you be ready for that moment when your twin flame finally comes into your life. And when they do, you will be giving them everything they are yearning for.

Who knows, your twin flame might be thinking about you right now. One of the characteristics that will unite you with the twin flame is a type of telepathic communication. This means that you don't even need to speak to them. They already know what you are feeling and vice-versa.

So, let's get started. Let's find out what we need to know in order to be ready for our twin flame.

Part I: What is a twin flame?

Chapter 1: Twin flames explained

> *"Our souls speak a language that is beyond human understanding. A connection so rare the universe won't let us apart."*
>
> *-- Nikki Rowe*

Our conversation will begin by discussing what a twin flame is. We will also discuss what a twin flame is not. It is important for you to make this clear distinction as it can be very easy to confuse a twin flame with an infatuation, a person whom you deeply care about, or just a wonderful human being who has played a significant role in your life.

In ancient Greek mythology, the famous philosopher Plato presented an idea about the origin of humans. Plato posed that in the beginning of the human race, there were three genders: male, female and androgynous. Male and female genders persist to this day, but androgyny does not.

Androgyny refers to one, single gender. It is not male nor female, but both. These androgynous humans were said to be of great strength and even posed a threat to the ancient Greek gods. So, the supreme god Zeus punished humans by splitting androgynous humans into two genders, male and female, for all eternity. This meant that humans that were once whole, now were two separate beings.

Then, Zeus cast humans down to Earth as part of the punishment. Humans would live forever yearning for their missing half. This also meant that humans had this inexplicable connection with someone. There would always be someone with whom they could immediately click. As such, part of their journey on Earth was to find this person.

Plato called them "soulmates."

This term refers to two beings who are meant to be together, a male and female component. However, we will see how Plato's idea of a soulmate go lost in translation.

What Plato was really talking about was a twin flame.

A twin flame is that soul that was split into two and then cast away onto the Earth. Since each half has been purposely placed away from the other, it is their mission to somehow find each other.

Now, the concept of a twin flame tends to be seen in a romantic context. Generally speaking, twin flames are considered to be lovers; to have a romantic relationship that leads to them uniting in deep and meaningful relationship. However, this isn't always the case.

A twin flame doesn't necessarily have to be a lover. This can be a family member, a dear friend or just someone whom you know that is the one that "gets you." In addition, the concept of a twin flame under a romantic context is generally portrayed as a male/female relationship.

Nevertheless, it is also quite possible for twin flames to be people of the same gender.

This is why you often have people who are miserable in heterosexual relationships but find bliss and joy in a same-sex relationship. So, even if a person's body is assigned a given gender, it doesn't mean that their soul is necessarily that particular gender.

Have you ever heard some folks say, "I am a woman trapped in a man's body?" Or the other way around?

Now, you have an answer.

As such, a twin flame is someone with whom you have a deep, spiritual connection that is just automatic. You can't explain it. In fact, it wouldn't make sense to explain it. You just know, instinctively, that this person is it.

If it is a lover, a romantic partner, then it is someone with whom you immediately click. It is someone that you feel you have known forever. You don't need to get to know this person; you already know them!

You have the same tastes, the same preferences, you have similar mannerisms, similar habits, well, you get the picture. This is why you often hear the term "mirror soul" when referring to a twin flame. As a matter of fact, the term "mirror soul" is quite apt.

Please bear in mind that this is not a person who is *like* you, this is a person who *is* you!

Your twin flame is the one that gets you. This is the person with whom you can't hide anything. They already know you and feel you. They understand everything that is going on in your mind. Often, you don't even have to say anything. They already understand what's happening inside your mind and your heart.

An encounter with a twin flame might look something like this:

You met at a place you both visit frequently. It could be a gym, a sports club, church, library, school, a place that you commonly visit. There are times when twin flames meet because they both work for the same company, but in different cities or even different countries. They meet at industry events because they do the same job. Or they meet as opponents.

Upon meeting this person, something automatically clicks. You already know who they are. This triggers that feeling of "have we met somewhere before?" Perhaps you have. Perhaps you have already met them, yet you can't put your finger on it.

Often, it is common for twin flames to meet at some point in their childhood or teenage years, then drift away only to be reunited for one reason or another.

If it is a romantic relationship that develops, there is instant attraction, instant chemistry. This isn't love at first sight. It is something a lot deeper than that. It is something so much more than finding a spark. In fact, you can find a spark with just about anyone you find physically attractive.

This is an instinctive, gut-feeling reaction that tells you that this is the one you have been waiting for all your life. You don't need to ask them out on a date; plans have already been made. You don't need to get their number and wait for a call; the line is already open.

What about an encounter with a twin flame that is not a romantic partner?

This example might surprise you: think about the military, yes, the military.

Hollywood films often portray soldiers in war as this inseparable group, a family if you will, that come from all different types of geographical locations, backgrounds and socioeconomic levels. Yet, they all have one thing in common: they will go off to war. Their training tells them that they need to rely on each other. Otherwise, they might very well be killed. These soldiers form a bond that is so close that there is nothing, nor anyone, who can separate them. They truly become brothers on the battlefield.

This bond is so strong that they remain lifelong friends even when their time in the military is up. They are friends who never leave each other. Even if they live in different cities, or different countries, they are always together, one way or another. The esteem and admiration between them run so deep that they cannot explain why they are so much in synch.

Then there is family.

Have you ever heard someone say that one of their parents totally gets them? It shouldn't surprise you that they might be talking about a twin flame.

How so?

It is quite common to see a parent and a child become so in synch, that parents instinctively know when their child is in distress, what they are going through and how they can reach them. Often, this parent-child relationship is a source of solace for the child even as an adult. On the flip side, there are children who tend to their parents in such a way that the relationship seems to be inverted. There are many times when adult children take care of their parents as if the roles had been reversed. The parent then feels like their child is the only one that truly gets them and understands them.

As you can see, a twin flame is not necessarily a romantic situation. In fact, it can take on many different facets. So, it might be that you have known your twin flame all your life, or it might be that they are still out there, waiting to be discovered.

Yet, the connection is still very much the same as is that feeling of peace and harmony when you are with that "mirror" of yourself.

Now, it is important to understand that a twin flame is not someone who is meant to take care of you. They are not a "guardian" or "protector." Some folks confuse a co-dependent relationship with a twin flame or a soulmate.

If you find yourself in a relationship in which you are receiving love and care, but you don't return an equal amount, then you might feel like the other person gets you and understand you, but the other party may not feel that in exchange.

Co-dependent relationships are usually based on one individual feeling vulnerable and helpless while the other feels like a champion, a savior, that must be there for the other person no matter what. So, this is a feedback loop that may never be broken.

Also, people confuse physical attraction and chemistry with finding a twin flame. This is also a false positive as intense physical relationships tend to fizzle out over time. As such, it is quite common to become confused by the affinity that may arise from a romantic and often sexual relationship.

In addition, it is easy to confuse a twin flame with someone with whom you have a common cause. For example, you meet in a political group, or perhaps you are activists; you believe in the same things and hold the same values. This affinity might lead you to think that you have found your twin flame, when in fact, you are just forming a bond with a like-minded individual.

Between twin flames, there is no need to have a common cause. There is no need to believe in the same things. And certainly, there is no need to have physical attraction. All of that is already built in. It is just there. There is no assembly required.

Furthermore, lonely individuals might end up mistaking virtually any relationship with a twin flame. This is usually the result of a desperate individual seeking love and companionship. So, when they find a person who takes a genuine interest in them, they might go in headlong thinking that this is it. However, they may ignore some of the warning signs that indicate that it is not the real thing.

Consequently, the purpose of a twin flame is to elevate your spiritual being. If you believe that a twin flame is something to be treasured and cherished here, on Earth, then you are only getting half the picture.

Plato was clear in his portrayal of "souls." He never said anything about bodies being split; it was souls that were split and set apart. As such, you are not searching for a physical connection. You are searching for a spiritual one.

Thus, your twin flame is meant to take you to the next spiritual level. Your flame will challenge you in ways no one has ever challenged you before. They won't humor you just because they don't want to upset you; they will upset you! They will push you to become a better person.

What does this mean?

It means that your twin flame will dare you to become the best version of yourself that you could possibly be.

That might mean that your twin flame will motivate you to go to the gym and get in shape. Your twin flame will encourage you to learn something new. Your twin flame will dare you to drop bad habits and pick up newer, healthier ones.

In short, a twin flame will bring out the best in you. They will never settle for a lesser version of you. They will always strive to get the best out of you.

Why?

It is simple: your twin flame wants the same thing for you as they want for themselves.

Think about that for a moment.

Truly selfless love always wants the best for the object of its affection. And it's not material possessions.

Hardly.

If your idea of winning over the object of your affection is through purchasing them material things, then you are way off base. Your twin flame will never care about the material possessions you can give them.

They want you!

Of course, providing a stable family life is at the core of a marriage but material possessions will never define your relationship. In fact, these types of romantic relationships are often characterized by those couples who don't need to go anywhere fancy or spend any money to be happy.

They simply enjoy each other's company.

Twin flames that are based on a friendship are the kind of friends who simply enjoy being with each other. They are the kind of friends who care and support each other in spite of their shortcomings. They are unconditional. They don't ask questions. In fact, most people often mistake them for siblings. Even if they are very different physically, most folks will believe they are related on some way.

When you are ready to meet up with your twin flame, you will find that you have made incredible gains as a person. You will notice that you are not the same person you were in the past. There is something about you that is different now. It is this new mindset, or perhaps an improved emotional state, that allows you to see your twin flame for who they are. Perhaps they have been right in front of you all this time. However, your personal baggage hasn't allowed you to see them.

Or perhaps it's the other way around. You are absolutely sure it is them, but they are in such a tough spot that they can't see the forest for the trees. That is where your role as a twin flame is to help your mirror soul become the best version they can be.

But please keep in mind that even if you do discover your twin flame, they may not end up being by your side 24/7. In fact, you might have such different lives, or come from such different backgrounds, that it might be impossible for you to be together.

A classic case of this is when two married people discover each other as their twin flame. Since they are already married, and more than likely have a family, leaving their spouses and families may end up being an insurmountable obstacle. So, rather than having a clandestine affair, they will part ways. And while they may remain in touch, the distance between is too far to bridge.

Yet, twin flames will always come back to each other. In one way or another they will always be together. Even if one of the two becomes a "runner" and the other the "chaser," they will always come back to each other. Twin flames cannot be apart. Since they are one, they will inevitably end up together again.

After all, their connection is not physical. It is spiritual. As such, it transcends everything in the material world. Therefore, they have a spiritual bond which cannot be severed by geographical distances. Twin flames will always be together at some deeper, much more meaningful level.

Chapter 2: The difference between soulmates and twin flames

"A big issue that some empaths face is unrequited love and all the grief that accompanies this experience. If someone truly is your soulmate or twin flame, the relationship will happen sooner or later. Don't put your life on hold for another person, no matter how badly you want to be with them. If it's meant to be, it will be."

-- Mateo Sol

Waiting for that special someone can feel like an eternity. The feeling of yearning and longing can seem like it has taken years away from your life. For some, life feels like a black hole until the one appears. Then, life suddenly has meaning; life suddenly has purpose.

In mainstream society, the concept of "soulmates" and "twin flames" is often confused. In fact, many folks seem to think that both terms refer to the same thing. The fact of the matter is that they are two completely different things.

In the previous chapter, we defined twin flames as one soul split in half. It is not two beings coming together to make one. It is one being becoming whole again. It is the reunion of two missing pieces. Hence, many cultures refer to spouses as "the other half."

A soulmate, however, is a person that will be with you throughout the course of your life, or perhaps just a brief period. A soulmate is more about companionship than a magical union. Soulmates are more like a buddy than part of your true purpose in life.

For instance, your spouse might very well be your soulmate. Your spouse is the person that has been with you through thick and thin. This is a person whom you love very deeply and cherish. You cannot live without this person. Nevertheless, they are not your twin flame.

How can you tell?

It's easy. How many married couples have you seen that spend 40 years together and still don't understand each other?

Perhaps your parents have a relationship like this.

Perhaps you have friends who have a love/hate relationship with their spouses.

Other times, you can see it in married couple who separate and get back together numerous times.

Soulmates can also be friends and relatives. They are people that are meant to be together in one way or another. And yes, you can have more than one soulmate.

What does that mean?

It means that a soulmate is more like a person who agrees to be with you for a given period of time. Now, they might be with you for your entire life, or they may be with you for a brief period. When they leave, it is because their purpose has been fulfilled.

In the case of a twin flame, they will never leave. Even if they are physically away, they will always be with you on a spiritual level.

As such, a soulmate works more like a contract. It is an agreement that two beings will be together for X amount of time. While the period of time may vary greatly, this other being agrees to be your companion until you have learned a lesson.

That is the main role of your soulmate.

They will help you learn that lesson. When the lesson has been learned, they will leave. Then, you might find another soulmate who will agree to join you for the rest of journey as you learn a new lesson or live through another experience.

If you think about it, it really makes sense.

This explains why there are people who come into your life, make a significant impact and then leave. There might be an abrupt separation, or there may just fade away. Nevertheless, there is something that separates you.

This is very common among lovers.

There are people who seem to be destined to be together. There is an instant attraction. The passion is intense, and then they fade away.

Sometimes, these relationships are born out of two people working together on a similar cause. Or, they just happen to be at the right place, at the right time. Then, the cause, project, job, school, or whatever brought them together, draws to a close. They vow that they will keep in touch and try their hardest to stay together, but then the passion fizzles out.

When these relationships occur, you often hear folks say things like, "he changed me" or "she helped me become a better person."

This quote sums up that feeling: "a soulmate is someone whose way of viewing life is not necessarily the same as yours but complements yours. There is not a compromise, there is a complement."

The previous quote by Paul Robear sums it up quite well.

Soulmates are two individuals who complement each other in incredible ways. One is the perfect fit for the other. They are each other's perfect counterpart. Where one is flawed or weak, the other picks up the slack.

Think about athletes.

It is very common to see two athletes playing on the same team. They know exactly how to complement each other in such a way that one helps the other be successful and vice-versa.

In the 1980s, the San Francisco 49ers football team had a dynamic duo in Joe Montana and Jerry Rice. Both are Hall of Fame players. They are considered the best quarterback-wide receiver duo in NFL history. They won four Super Bowls together. They complemented each other perfectly well on the field. Sure, there were other players on the field, but it was Montana and Rice who made the magic happen.

Both Montana and Rice would go on to play on different teams. However, they will always be remembered for their time together on the 49ers squad. Their legend persists to this day. And without a doubt, they are an example of how two completely different individuals can come together, for a common cause, and become incredibly close. And then, their time together expires, and they move on to a different part of their lives.

Both Montana and Rice would go on to have success with their new teams. They became a positive influence on the players on those teams. You could say that they had lessons to share with the other players who need their guidance and experience.

This story, about two football players, illustrates how soulmates don't necessarily need to be lovers. They can be two great friends who share an unbreakable bond. But their time together isn't meant to be forever.

Twin flames, on the other hand, don't complement each other. They are not different individuals that come together for a cause and then go their separate ways. They are two parts of the same person. They are completely in synch. They don't need to get acquainted and they don't need to become used to each other.

Twin flames are on the same mission. They are after the same goals and the same purpose. While they may come from different walks of life, their path and their goals are the same.

One such example is a twin flame couple that works on medical missions in Africa. Their purpose is to deliver aid and health care to some of the poorest people in the world. They are not doctors nor do they play the same role. One works in administration while the other works in fundraising. They work with different organizations. Yet, they met on a mission. Their attraction was instantaneous. Sure, this is a couple that eventually married, but despite the differences in what they actually do for a living, they shared the same cause.

This couple does not complement each other. They do the same thing. They help needy people get the treatment they need.

In this example, it is clear to see how twin flames often push each other to become better, to improve themselves, to further their cause. They had to inevitably meet somewhere, at some point, and help each other grow spiritually.

A soulmate relationship would have put both of these beings to aid each other in learning a lesson. And once their time together was over, they would go on to the next phase in their lives.

At this, you might be wondering: how can I tell the difference?

And that is a valid point. You might be thinking about that special someone in your life, but you might be confused.

Here is a simple, but effective exercises which you can do in order to get a response from the most reliable of sources you can find: your heart.

This exercise has seven steps and requires you to tune into your heart. You need to be in tune with your spiritual being. That inner voice that speaks to you in your moments of quiet and solitude needs to come out. It has the answer that you are yearning to hear.

Find a quiet place. Your bedroom, living room, garden, anywhere where you can be at peace, on your own. Please turn off your phone, no music, not even a running fountain. This exercise needs full concentration.

Now, imagine a bright ball of light engulfing you; all of you. You can imagine this as a flame or just a beacon of light. This light is meant to represent the light at the core of the Earth, the light at the core of the universe.

The next step is to breathe. Take deep breaths. Inhale and exhale. Each breath is meant to align your spiritual being with your physical body. As you inhale, count from 1 to 5. This will help your lungs become filled with air. This air provides rich oxygen to your cells. Then, hold your breath for a moment. You can count from 1 to 3. After, exhale. As you exhale, count from 1 to 5. This will help empty your lungs.

As you breathe and become more in tune with your feelings, picture that ball of light completely enveloping you. As you achieve a state of relaxation, ask the question. Ask your heart to show the truth, the reality of what you wish to know. Is that special someone your twin flame? Are they a soulmate?

Now, visualize that person standing in front of you. Imagine what they look like. Picture all the little nuances about them. Their physical characteristics, their facial expressions, even the little quirks that make them who they are. Picture this loved one reach out to you, as if to embrace you. You may do this, too, if you wish.

As you reach out to each other, picture your hearts touching, literally. How does that feel? How does it feel when your hearts are coming together? What feelings do you get? A clear indication is a magnetic attraction which you cannot escape. You cannot explain it. It just happens that way. You might even become invaded by feelings of joy, wholeness and bliss.

Try to capture that feeling you are getting. Try to capture those emotions and put them in your heart. Imagine that you can curl them up into a ball and deposit them in the center of your chest. Let them sink in. Pay attention to what your heart is telling you. What does it say? More importantly, what do you feel? These are the answers you need.

This is a great visualization exercise which can help you wrap your mind around your feelings. It will help you get a grasp of your feelings and your thoughts. You don't need any fancy technologies or fortune tellers telling you the truth. All of the answers you need are in your heart.

After all, why would someone else tell you what you feel?

There is no one in the universe who can tell you what you feel. You are the only judge of that.

Don't worry if you don't get the answer you need on your first try. Often, it is not easy to tune into your heart especially if you have never done an exercise such as this before. It usually takes time and practice. Nevertheless, your heart will always try to speak to you. It might be that you get the answer you are looking for when you least expect it. It might come to you at a moment where your mind is calm, at ease.

If you believe that you haven't met your twin flame yet, you can do the same exercise. But instead of visualizing the person you think is your twin flame, ask your heart to reveal this person to you. This is a means of establishing that connection with your twin flame. You will be calling out to them. You will attempt to establish this link.

Try calling out to your twin flame. You can send out signals. Ask them where they are. Ask them to get in touch with you. The likelihood of them looking for you is quite high, too. Perhaps they are not making the same conscious effort that you are, but your call will surely find them.

Please bear in mind that twin flames are connected on a very deep, instinctive, spiritual level. So, there is nothing between you. There is nothing that will impede the bond of communication between each other. There is a direct line which nothing can sever.

A soulmate, on the other hand, will not respond to you in the same manner. If you call out to them, they might reply, though you will have to work hard to establish that connection. While it is not impossible, developing a deep and lasting connection with a soulmate takes some work.

Of course, your soulmate will also be drawn to you. They will seek out to find you. They will come into your life when the moment is right. And while you may both have an instant connection, you will know in your heart that they are not your twin flame. There will always be something about them that won't resonate on the same level.

In fact, soulmates often produce a sense of "being on the same wavelength" but they often lack that incredible and amazing sensation of overlapping energies. You might also get that feeling that your soulmate is someone you have known forever. This is why it is often easy to confuse a soulmate with a twin flame.

Please remember that you are the only one who can truly identify your twin flame. There is no magic out there which can tell you or reveal to you who this person is, or if you have already met them. The only way that you can find out is by listening to your heart. In this world that is filled with distractions and uncertainty, the answers that you need in your life are there, inside you, inside your heart. You don't need to go anywhere else.

So, please take the time to listen to your deeper self. Take the time to listen to what your soul has to say. Your soul will provide you with the assurance that you need.

Chapter 3: A twin flame for everyone

"A wounded heart that loves even more is immortal, it only survives and blooms time after time. If you happen to live in it, there's no safer place in the world than its beating."

-- Nicola An

The biggest question that arises in the minds of people is: is there a twin flame for everyone?

Do I have my own twin flame?

If so, when will I find him/her?

The answer to that question has a short and a long answer.

First, let's start with the short answer.

Does everyone have a twin flame? The answer is yes and no.

As a matter of fact, there is a very simple argument for yes.

Based on common lore (such as Plato's beliefs) and the understanding of humans' spiritual beingness, yes, unequivocally, there is a twin flame for everyone.

This argument is predicated upon the fact that twin flames are one soul that was split apart. Thus, there are two sides to this coin. One needs to find the other. Therefore, the answer is a resounding yes.

Your twin flame is around, somewhere, waiting to reunite with you. Your twin flame is actively seeking you, whether they are aware of it, or not. You see, being born into this world, the dimension of consciousness has its advantages and its drawbacks.

For starters, being born on this planet provides souls with a great opportunity to learn and grow. The lessons that we have the opportunity to learn are invaluable to growth and spiritual development. Even the most painful experiences have the potential for growth and understanding.

However, we tend to get caught up in the hustle and bustle of our daily lives. We have so many distractors out there that it might seem virtually impossible to sort things out. It seems almost impossible to see where we are headed and why we are going where we are.

That being said, there is an instinctive, unconscious pursuit of the other half. It just makes sense. You can't expect your other half to just sit by idly waiting for life to happen. There is something a lot deeper that will push you to seek out that other half of your soul.

Otherwise, why would you have this yearning, this longing to find that perfect match, that perfect fit?

Indeed, there is a twin flame out there for everyone.

Now, there is a reason why there is a no.

The simple reason for no is that your twin flame may not have been born yet or they may have passed on already.

In fact, it is a lot more common for twin flames to live in different timelines in history. It all boils down to the conscious decision to come to this Earth at a given point in time. While this decision runs a lot deeper, the fact that you might have been born before or after your twin flame comes to Earth can wreak havoc on your emotions.

It could be that your twin flame hasn't even been born yet. Or, it might be that you arrived just after they passed on. Whatever the circumstance, it just means that your twin flame is not physical around at this time.

But that doesn't mean they don't exist.

It just means that you won't be able to meet them physically during your lifetime.

Of course, this concept is rooted in the idea of reincarnation and multiple incarnations. If we choose to go down that road, the idea of multiple existences with your twin flame comes into focus. It explains why you know this being so well. It provides clarity into why you both know each other so very well.

But what about soulmates? Don't they also meet over the course of various lifetimes?

Yes, that is also true. Soulmates have long-time contracts in which they pledge to be together for various existences. But then again, it is a pledge, a deal, an agreement, a contract, whatever you want to call it. It is not the other half of your being.

Do you see where this leads?

We are not talking about someone who has agreed to join you at various stages in your journey. We are talking about someone who is simply "it" or "the one."

This last point isn't meant to discourage you. Rather, it is meant to bring both sides of this argument into focus. If you don't see both sides to this question, then you are doing yourself a disservice. You are essentially cutting yourself out from reality. And yes, it is a real possibility that your twin flame isn't here…yet.

Earlier, we mentioned that there was a long answer to this question. As such, let's take a look at three important arguments which will give you a deeper understanding of the question of there being a twin flame for you.

Argument #1: Twin flames exist at the same time though not in the same physical location

This first argument plays into the concept of your twin flame not being incarnated yet.

So, yes, we all have a twin flame out there somewhere.

Let's also assume that they have been born in the same timeline as us. Though there might be a discrepancy in the actual time of incarnation (for instance, one might be considerably older than the other) the biggest limitation might be the geographical location of each half.

Even if we assumed that your twin flame was born on the same day, in the same month, of the same year (thereby both of you having the exact same birthdate), but if you were born in completely different locations in the world, then the odds of you meeting would be stacked against.

Let's assume the following scenario:

You were born in a middle-class family living in a developed nation. You had access to all the comforts the First World has to offer upper-income families. You had a solid family with a decent upbringing, access to quality health care and good schooling. Your parents genuinely loved you, took care of you and provided for you. You went to a good college, got a good job out of college and have now replicated your family's middle-class status. You live in your own apartment, have a great social life, are active in several causes, but there is something missing.

The people you have dated, while some great and others not so, don't fill you up in the way you'd hope or expect them to. They don't appeal to your life's purpose. Sure, there might be some great attraction and spark, but they just aren't the one who will make your head spin.

Now, let's suppose that your twin flame was born in a Third World country. They grew up in one of the poorest countries in the world. A country that has little to no rule of law. The country might have even been ravaged by war. They didn't have the same opportunity to go to school, they have worked since they were a small child and had parents who didn't really take care of them.

It's also safe to say they don't have the same opportunity to travel the world. Most likely, your twin flame hasn't even been very far from their village or town. It is highly unlikely that you even speak the same language or have a similar culture.

So, the question begs: how could you ever possibly meet?

While there exists a strong spiritual and emotional connection between the two of you, the likelihood of one of you travelling to the same place, the same geographical location is rather hard. Even if you meet in a neutral site, how likely would that be?

What if things were the other way around?

What if your twin flame lived in a First World country and you were living in a Third World country located in a different continent?

This alone may cause you to be apart during this existence.

Eventually, you might end up settling on a great person (perhaps a soulmate) while your twin flame may very well succumb to social conventions and marry someone, too. Your lives would be completely different and thereby kill the chances of you meeting.

In this scenario, we are assuming that this is a romantic relationship. Of course, there are cases of twin siblings, who separated at birth, spend a lifetime looking for each other. There are cases where individuals are fixated on finding a long-lost parent. Or perhaps they are looking for a childhood friend with whom they have lost contact.

Indeed, twin flames can come in any configuration. Your heart will be the one to tell you the difference.

Even if you were both in the same city, on the exact same moment in time, but lived on different streets, just the fact that you grew up in different families opens the door for N possibilities for divergence. Your parents would make certain choices that would affect your life while your twin flame's parents would make choices that would affect their lives. Simply based on that, the likelihood of you meeting would become skewed to the opposite direction.

This is why your heart will give you the right answer. If you believe you have met this person, then you will know if they are really the one.

Argument #2: Issues recognizing a twin flame

Recognizing a twin flame would be very easy if they lived in the same city as you, had a similar lifestyle and did many of the same things you did.

Under these circumstances, it would be far easier to pinpoint your twin flame. You wouldn't have to be open-minded and accept that this person is your twin flame.

Again, we are assuming a romantic relationship.

However, things get complicated when your twin flame does not live under the same circumstances as you.

Would you recognize if your twin flame was dirt poor while you were filthy rich?

Would you recognize your twin flame if you were an ordinary citizen and they were a famous celebrity?

Would you be able to recognize your twin flame if you didn't even speak the same language?

These are questions which invariably come into play. You cannot expect to pick out your twin flame out of crowd.

If only it were that easy.

Even if you had your twin flame right in front of you, right now, staring back at you, how would you know that they were the one?

One of the most common mistakes that people make is believing that their twin flame has to be a lover. In fact, a twin flame can be virtually anyone in this life. In reality, your twin flame just wants to be with you, to come together and fulfill a higher spiritual purpose.

When you think about it, fulfilling that deeper spiritual purpose does not necessarily imply that you might be lovers. In fact, you might marry your soulmate but have your twin flame play a different role in your life.

Take the example of Truman Capote and Harper Lee.

They are both giants in the world of literature. They were both exceptionally gifted writers. They both pushed each other to become better. They both pursued the same level of excellence in their field. Yet, they were friends. Despite being opposite genders, they were lifelong friends. They grew up together in Monroeville, Alabama. They had similar lives and similar destinies.

And while their claim to fame came in different literary genres, both of their life's works are considered to be a testament to the genius of the human spirit. They both credited each other with contributing to the success of each other's work. It is known that Truman helped Harper get through writing *To Kill a Mockingbird* by coaching her to improve your writing skills. On the flip side, Harper pushed Truman through the writing of *In Cold Blood*, especially when the details of the case got too gory and too sordid for Truman.

Harper Lee won the Pulitzer for *To Kill a Mocking Bird* in 1961, while *In Cold Blood* is considered to be a groundbreaking work that led to the creation of the true crime genre and the rise of investigative journalism.

This is a wonderful example of how two individuals can push each other to become better people, better at their field and walk along the same line.

You might argue that they were simply soulmates. That would be a valid argument though there is one simple difference. A soulmate would have supported one through the ordeal they had to face in order to become great. In this case, they not only supported each other, they did the same job and their fierce competitiveness helped them excel in their chosen field.

Truman Capote passed on in 1984 while Harper Lee left us in 2016.

Argument #3: You are not ready for your twin flame

This one is a biggie.

Meeting your twin flame is one thing. Actually, being ready for your twin flame is another. Your twin flame is your mirror image. They are on the same mission as you are. They are on the same path as you. They are looking to fulfill the same purpose as you.

But, do you know what that purpose is?

Do you know what path you are headed on?

It is very important for you to know and understand that your twin flame is there to walk alongside with you on that path. But it might be that you are simply not ready to be with them yet. You need to reach a place within yourself in which you can support and push your twin flame to become the best that both of you can become.

Do you feel ready to be everything that your twin flame needs you to be?

Think about that for a moment.

Imagine this scenario.

What would the perfect person for you be like?

What traits would they have?

What would they have to do in order for them to be the perfect fit for you?

Now, turn those questions on yourself. If you were to become your ideal partner, would you be the person that would be the best fit for you?

In other words, would you be the partner that you would like for yourself?

That is a rather complex question. You might have to think long and hard about that one. But by being honest and answering that question truthfully, you will be able to identify areas and aspects about yourself that you feel you would have to improve. As you realize those areas for improvement, it will become clear to you that your twin flame is expecting you to be at the top of your game.

While this doesn't mean that even if you are going through a rough patch you won't be able to find your twin flame, it does mean that you might be in a situation that is holding you back.

Later on in this book, we will take a closer look at the potential obstacles that are holding you back from becoming the best version of yourself. Often, some of these adverse situations may keep you from finding and recognizing your twin flame.

Chapter 4: Twin flames are meant to be lovers

"He was the one I wasn't looking for."

-- Nikki Rowe

Let's take some time to explore this issue further.

Earlier we have stated that twin flames don't always have to be lovers. In fact, they could have any type of relationship. However, the most common type of relationship between twin flames is that of lovers.

As such, we need to take some time to dig deeper into this issue so that you can be clear on the type of relationship you might have with your twin flame.

There are many factors that play into your relationship with your twin flame. Given that human existence is rather complicated, there might by any number of circumstances which could dictate the type of relationship between you and your twin flame.

As you become clear on the type of factors that come into play, you will gain a better understanding of how, and why, things are the way they are. As you learn to navigate through these issues, you can gain a better appreciation for your reality and that of your twin flame.

Furthermore, it generally requires a great deal of maturity and self-discovery in order to understand where you and your twin flame are coming from. That will allow you to put your union into perspective so that you can both walk along the same path and become tuned into your purpose in life; into the things you are meant to be doing together as a part of your journey down this path of life.

Factor #1: Age

This has got to be the biggest question that arises with would-be twin flames.

In the case of lovers, this tends to be a big issue. For instance, what would be a normal age gap? How would this apply if one was considerably older?

There are a lot of social taboos that might come into play here. While it would be fine for a man to be considerably older than a woman, would it cause uncertainty if it was the other way around? If this were the case, then a romantic relationship may not be possible due to social and cultural norms. A large age gap may lead to family questioning your decision. As such, a large age gap might be too much to take for a romantic relationship.

Indeed, a considerable age might cause you to doubt whether the person you feel is your twin flame truly is your flame. If the age gap is greater than 20 years, then you might be a little bit off base. Nevertheless, a 20-year age gap, either way, shouldn't surprise you. It is just the way that twin flames choose to come into this world.

If you have an age gap that is greater than 20 years, then you might find that a relationship in which the elder is a mentor and the younger is a protégé would work out best. This can happen with folks of the same gender in which one acts more like a father/mother figure. Also, you will find that an older individual will take the younger individual under their wing.

These cases can be seen in those folks who never had children of their own and suddenly meet a child or teenager that has be abandoned. They know they are not related, but they act in that way. They form a deep and lasting bond that transcends their understanding.

So, don't let age throw you off. It might just be that you are not looking for a lover, but rather, someone you truly need.

Factor #2: Marital status

What if one, or both you, were already married?

This can put a serious damper on any romantic relationship. Nevertheless, it does lead to individuals having extramarital affairs because their attraction is so deep.

Now, this isn't to say that you should act on your feelings, especially if this will cause you to risk ruining your marriage and your family. Nevertheless, most twin flames do have some type of romance at some point in their union. Even if it is a harmless relationship in which there is no physical contact, the other will become that emotional rock particularly in times when a spouse doesn't fit the bill.

In fact, this is one of the reasons why a person has a "work spouse."

A work spouse is a platonic relationship in which two colleagues, usually working in the same office or same company, will come to depend on each other in much the same way they would rely on their regular spouse.

While there is attraction and chemistry, their bond is purely platonic. They will not act on their feelings by engaging in a physical or sexual relationship. They will just lean heavily on each other for emotional and spiritual support.

The work spouse may become the shoulder to cry on, or the helping hand in times of need. Yet, when work is out, their relationship is also out. They have their own families and their own obligations. Nevertheless, that emotional and spiritual connection is always there.

Of course, there are times when one, or both, twin flames leave their spouse and have a relationship of their own. These circumstances do happen, though they are not as often as you might imagine. So, if you are married, or your suspected flame is also married and/or in a long-term relationship, think long and hard if a romance is best. Perhaps just having a platonic relationship might be the best solution.

Factor #3: Culture

There are times when culture does get in the way of two flames. Think about those cultures that may put some kind of restriction on romantic relationship such as cultures that frown upon two people of different social classes having a relationship.

There are times when two people of different religious, or ethnic, groups may also meet with resistance. It is not uncommon for individuals to meet such resistance especially when there are serious limitations in the way.

Think about the classic love story of Romeo and Juliet. They were two young people who were deeply in love with one another. Yet, they met resistance because their families were mortal enemies. They went against the odds and decided they were going to be together anyhow. Despite the resistance from their families, they lived out their passion.

In the end, the story ends as all good Shakespearean dramas do: Romeo and Juliet both drink poison at the thought that their beloved had died.

You might be thinking, "Romeo and Juliet is just a story; it's not the real thing."

Well, think about street gangs.

Street gangs usually have a rival group with whom they are sworn enemies. To them, the opposite gang is the enemy. And so, they must exterminate their mortal enemies. Yet, there are stories of two members of opposite gangs who fall in love. Some of them die at the hands of the rival gangs. Others escape; they run away together, fleeing their gangs.

Indeed, culture can play a huge role in stopping twin flames from becoming lovers. Yet, there are plenty of stories out there of happy couples who have defied the odds and ended up together despite the hardships they faced.

Factor #4: Gender

This is a bit of a gray area.

If we assume that twin flames have romantic relationships, where does that put same-sex relationships?

There's an easy answer to that, and it's that it doesn't matter. A twin flame is a twin flame. Perhaps both of you decided to live that experience prior to coming to this Earth. Perhaps you felt that by being in a same-sex relationship you could learn something, improve upon yourself in a way that you wouldn't have been able as a heterosexual couple.

The problem with such a relationship is the amount of potential social and cultural resistance that you might meet. This is especially true in cultures where such relationships are condemned. Nevertheless, you often find that couples who really and deeply love each other will do what it takes to be together.

Other times, their romantic feelings do not go beyond a profound and meaningful relationship. On the surface, they are just good friends. But on a deeper level, their feelings go far beyond that of just friends.

The truth of the matter is that gender, just like age or culture, does not affect the feelings of the twin flames; they are just the layers of social and cultural pressure that have been formed over time. And while now it is easier than ever to have a same-sex relationship, there is still a long way to go.

Please don't feel down if this is you. If you have found your twin flame, regardless of gender, then you have found one of the most marvelous things any human can find. You have found an incredible treasure. So, you must cherish it and value it for what it is. Such treasures are not found lying around on the street. They are the result of your work to improve yourself, to be the type of being that your twin flame needs you to be.

One of the keys to being ready for your twin flame is acceptance. Ultimately, if your social group doesn't accept you, it pales in comparison to accepting yourself. After all, what good does it do if everyone accepts you and approves of you, but you feel miserable?

The bottom line

When it comes to twin flame relationships, there is nothing that says that it has to be a romantic relationship. The experience of being with your twin flame is one of bliss, joy and happiness. That is why there is no set format for the way it should be. It can take any shape. It can happen at any time, and it can certainly end.

The good news about that is that you will be destined to find each other one way or another. It is the purpose of the twin flames to find each other. However, the two separate portions of the same soul cannot just reunite at the drop of a hat.

The reunion between twin flames is a process that takes time and dedication on both ends. While one half might be farther along than the other, it doesn't mean that they can't be together. In fact, the two parts might agree to come together because they need to take that next step forward in unison.

On the contrary, it might be that the two parts decide they need time apart in order to work on lessons that they still haven't learned; the ones they are yet to master. As a matter of fact, the time spent apart helps strengthen that bond between the two halves of the twin flame.

How so?

The bond is strengthened because the only thing keeping you together is that spiritual link, that spiritual connection that transcends everything in this world. And while you may be very happy and very comfortable with your soulmate or life partner, a part of you is still yearning for that other half. You may have everything you have ever wanted in life, but at the end of the day, you still feel incomplete.

Take the time to go over your current relationships, friends, family, partners, lovers, and even your enemies. You may find clues as to your fate, your destiny in those relationships. It might be that you find that your twin flame has been there all along. Yet, you have been caught up in so many other things that you haven't noticed it.

Perhaps your twin flame is still far away from you. Or better yet, they might be just around the corner. Whatever the case, there is only one way you can find out. Only you have the answers to those very important questions. Only you have the knowledge and the wisdom to read what's inside your heart.

The journey to finding your twin flame isn't easy. It almost never is. It is filled with ups and downs. But in the end, it is absolutely worth any pain and suffering you may have to go through to get there. That is why this book is about helping you improve yourself; to become the best version that you could possibly become.

....and twin flames come and go

One of the characteristics of twin flames, regardless of the type of relationship, is that they come in and out of your life. Now, don't look at this in terms of weeks, months or years. Look at this in terms of various lifetimes. Look at this in the grander scheme of the universe.

If you look at how your twin flame comes and goes, you will realize that they never leave you. They just step out for a moment and then re-enter your life with a fresh perspective on things. Since you both need to experience the various experiences that life has to offer, you may not always be on the same path at the same time. But whatever road you take, it will lead you back to them.

There is also one very important factor that you need to keep in mind. Humans have free will. That means that we have the opportunity to decide what we are going to do with our lives while we are here on this planet. We get to decide what we are going to every single day or our lives.

One such example is this book. You could have decided to do anything else with your time. Yet, we are here, having this discussion. You made the choice to listen to this message. It was your time to listen to this message now – not before, nor tomorrow. It had to be today.

Now, please bear in mind that your twin flame also has the same option to make the same type of choices based on their free will. So, don't blame them for making choices which don't necessarily lead to you. It might just be that they need time away from you to find themselves, learn more about what they need to be. Perhaps you are ready for them, but they just aren't ready for you.

It might just be that the time you continue to spend apart will only lead you to have a blissful existence once you are reunited. And yes, fireworks will go off, even if you are just friends or even family. But the time you spend together will be the time that you cherish and treasure for the rest of your lives.

If you have found your twin flame, if you know who we are talking about, then don't push them. The last thing you want to be with your twin flame is possessive. They love you just as much as you love them. You don't need to be possessive. They will always come back to you. They may spend some time away and even with other folks, but make no mistake, they will choose you every day of the week and twice on Sunday.

Part II: Making it easier to find your twin flame

Chapter 5: Getting yourself ready for a reunion

"When you find your twin flame you also find your freedom, for there is nothing more exhilarating, wild and free than absolute soul love."

-- Melody Lee

Now that you have a clear idea of what a twin flame is and what it is not, we need to move on to a very important part of the process. In fact, this is a pivotal part of the journey that will lead you to your twin flame.

This part of the journey is generally filled with many ups and downs, pitfalls and other obstacles along the way. We all fall over these obstacles from time to time. Yet, there is something that always keeps us going. There is something that doesn't let us quit. There is a little voice inside your head that won't let you give up even when you are ready to throw in the towel.

The famous survivalist and outdoorsman Bear Grylls put it best: "Survival can be summed up in three words – never give up. That's the heart of it really. Just keep trying."

Wise words.

Survival in life is about moving. It is about not giving up when others would have better sense to do so than you. But that drive, that passion will not let you give up on yourself.

You have been through a lot and yet you are still here. You are still standing before the eyes of the universe. There are times when you feel that life has thrown everything at you, even the kitchen sink, but it can't break you down.

It is this attitude, this mindset, this willpower, that keeps you going. It keeps you thinking about how important it is for you to keep working on and improving yourself.

Why wouldn't you?

After all, the best investment you can make is to invest in yourself. You will never lose time, money or effort. It will always be there. It will always be there when you need it. It is never going to go down in value. If anything, it will become more valuable and more precious over time. It will pay off enormous dividends that money, gold or any of the riches in the world could ever pay off.

This is why the journey toward finding true happiness and joy, the kind that lies with a reunion with your twin flame is called "wholeness."

Your personal journey, the kind of journey that leads to the best version of yourself ends when you become a whole person, one, single being that is capable of taking on the world... and win.

For some, it has taken longer than others. To you, it might seem like a lifetime, but make no mistake, this isn't your first rodeo. You have been here many times before. Except this time, it really is different. This time you have everything you need to become successful in achieving the most important thing you could ever achieve: total and complete oneness.

Concept of wholeness

But what is wholeness?

What does it mean?

What does it imply?

Is it some type of nirvana?

Wholeness is a state in which an individual achieves peace, harmony and unity with themselves. In other words, the individual, the person, the being is at their natural self. It is a sign of completeness.

You might think, "but I am whole. I'm not missing any limbs and I still haven't lost my mind."

Yes, that is true. However, most of us live in a situation in which we are fragmented. We are not entirely whole. We are not entirely at peace and harmony. Our minds, spirits and emotions are either broken or damaged.

There are many ways in which a person can become broken or damaged emotionally. Please bear in mind that broken or damaged is not synonymous with being "insane" or "mentally ill." When a person is mentally ill, it is because they have a serious condition that warrants treatment. They are a recognized condition that goes beyond the usual aches and pains that everyone goes through in life.

If you have suffered some of these aches and pains, some of the events that can severely cause you to become broken or damaged emotionally, your emotions can become out of whack. They can be so severely damaged that you may not function properly. Then, you are not really acting yourself. What you are doing is "playing through the pain."

Think about top-level athletes. They need to be in peak physical condition in order to become successful at what they do. But what happens if they become injured? They have to take a break and recover.

As a matter of fact, injuries are a perfectly normal part of sports. Of course, there are some that are harder than others. Sometimes injuries might be light sprains and muscle aches. Other times they are so severe that they threaten an athlete's career.

However, why does it make perfect sense in the world to sit an athlete down because of a physical injury, but we are forced to play through the pain of an emotional injury?

If you get hurt playing tennis, everyone will understand if you take a couple of weeks off to rest. Everyone will tell you that you made the right call.

When you get hurt emotionally, no one really seems to notice. And even if they did, they don't immediately tell you to take a step back and heal. Quite the opposite; we are expected to push through. We are expected to deal with it and move on.

One of the worst pieces of advice you could ever get it, "time heals all wounds."

News flash: time doesn't always heal all wounds.

If anything, time allows wounds to fester. Time allows wounds to become infected and simply get bigger and bigger.

But we don't do much about them. We just tend to cover them with layers of entertainment, trips, outings, activities, social clubs and what have you. We become fragmented because our mind and body are not in complete synch.

How many people have you seen that are in optimal physical condition, who have a body to envy, yet they are miserable inside?

Often, some of the most beautiful people you will see in the world (on the outside) are some of the saddest people on the inside (emotionally). After all, it is easier to cultivate a good-looking exterior than it is to cultivate a fully integrated being.

The first step to achieving wholeness

The first step that we must all take in achieve wholeness, oneness, in life is to accept ourselves. If you cannot accept yourself, if you cannot love yourself, then it will be virtually impossible for you to love someone else. Even your twin flame will be met with resistance and opposition if you cannot love yourself and accept who you are.

That is why the first step is to realize who you are.

Think about that for a moment.

If someone asked you, "who are you?" What would you reply?

What would you say to them?

Don't reply something like, "I am a computer scientist." No, that's your job.

Who are you?

Are you comfortable saying who you really are inside?

Here's another news flash: there is nothing wrong with who you are. There is nothing that's bad or inadequate about who you are. You are just you. If others don't want to accept you for who you are, then that's their business. You can't control that. You can't control what others think and feel. That is entirely up to them.

The only thing that you can control is the way you feel, the way you act, they way you react to yourself. Everything else comes in second.

Here's a great exercise that is so simple yet complicated. It is complicated in its simplicity.

Get a blank notebook. A nicely decorated notebook will work best. This is going to become your journal. This is going to become your new spiritual log. You might be tempted to use a tablet or smartphone for this, but what we are tying to avoid is the distraction of electronic devices. That is why plain paper will work best for this.

Now, atop a blank page write, "WHO AM I?"

Write that in big, capital letters.

Then, make a list of all the words that you feel describe you. Don't hold back. They can be either negative or positive. They can be either good or bad. Remember that we all have our good side and our bad side.

Also, it doesn't matter if you fill several pages. That's beside the point. You can fill out the entire notebook if you want. The point is to get your mind and your ideas flowing.

After you feel that you have written down enough words (or perhaps phrases), go back and reread everything you wrote down. Feel free to cross out words that don't really agree with and also add new ones that you might have missed.

Once you have a list which you are satisfied with, go back and look through it one more time. Try to see if you can spot any patterns or if any words jump at you. For example, you might notice that your positive traits are related to be kind and generous. Perhaps your negative traits are mostly related to your physical appearance.

Try to spot these patterns. Those patterns are there. They are there. They are a part of your consciousness becoming printed onto paper. It is a representation of what you truly feel. Don't hold back. Since this is a personal exercise, you don't need to be shy. This is for your eyes only.

As you detect these patterns, you will begin to learn things about yourself which you may or may not have really thought of before.

Please remember that this notebook can become a journal for you. It can become a chronicle of how you have evolved from one point to another. It can serve as a means of telling you that you have progressed throughout from the time you heard this message till the time you find your twin flame.

Becoming the best version of yourself

Becoming the best version of yourself may sound somewhat vague. It doesn't fully encompass everything that implies truly improving yourself and becoming a better version of who you are. In fact, it is hard to picture yourself as that new and improved version.

For starters, how would you look like if you were actually better?

How could you tell?

What aspects would make you such a better person?

It all begins with who you want to be. The journey to becoming the best version of yourself begins with finding the ultimate goal for you.

Let's begin by visualizing that new you.

This is a great visualization exercise similar to the one we did earlier. We can do it in 5 easy steps.

The first step is to find a quiet place. Bedrooms do well. But a comfortable chair in your living room, garden or even somewhere close to water. Water has a great deal of energy which you can share. If you are near the woods, the energy and positive vibration given off by nature is certainly an enhancer to your own abilities.

Next, close your eyes and breathe. Inhale and exhale. Each time you do, try your best to keep you back upright. Don't slouch over as that obstructs the passages in your lungs and throat. You can sit cross-legged if you are sitting on the floor or just with your hands on your lap if you are sitting on the floor.

Now, visualize yourself as you are. If it helps, take a long look at yourself in the mirror before trying this exercise. Give yourself a good look. Stare at yourself trying to take in as much of your physical and even spiritual self. Try to have that image engraved in your mind.

Once you can visualize that first impression of yourself, take the time to slowly morph aspects about yourself you'd like to change. Perhaps you are a bit overweight, perhaps you'd like to gain weight. Perhaps you'd like to hit the gym a little more. Maybe you would feel better about changing your hair, maybe even your wardrobe. Don't hold back. Then think about the non-physical things you would like to change about yourself. Think about your personality. The way you conduct yourself. It might be that you are shy or too impulsive. Think about all those things about your character and your personality that you would like to change. As this exercise takes shape you will begin to see the changes in yourself. You are not just imagining what you will be. You are actually becoming it!

As you begin to come out of this meditative state, don't just pop back up. Take the time to soak up everything that you have just seen. Take the time to internalize it. As you open your eyes and begin to move about, don't let go of that feeling you just had. Try your best to hold on to it as much as possible. Then, go back to the mirror. Only this time, be sure to look at yourself in the new light; in the light of your visualization. Please keep in mind that if you can see something, you will be able to do it; to become it.

As you can see, visualization is a powerful exercise. It is used by professional athletes and performers. When they are getting ready for a game or a show, they visualize themselves completing their performance or making the plays they need to make in the game.

One such example is media mogul Oprah Winfrey. From Oprah's humble beginnings, she was determined to become the best possible version of herself. Through the years, she has had her share of ups and downs. Yet, she has lived with the conviction of making her life as great as it possibly can be.

Over the years, Oprah has shared her visualization techniques with her followers. It isn't just about thinking that you can do something. It's about actually seeing yourself doing. She has said to her viewers and followers on numerous occasions, "create the highest, grandest vision possible for your life because you become what you believe."

Indeed, she is right. You become what you believe. If there is something which you believe you can do, something which you believe you can be, you will become it. If you don't believe it to be possible, then the chances of it actually happening are virtually null.

So, take the time to visualize what you want to be. Go through your day thinking about how you will improve and the things you will achieve. As long you firmly believe that anything is possible, then you will be amazed at how far a little positive thinking can go.

The power of affirmations

Have you ever heard someone say, "I have bad luck" and then something bad happens to them? Then you hear, "See? I have bad luck!"

That is an example of the power of affirmations.

If your mind's eye is powerful, your mouth is even stronger.

By saying things out loud, you are automatically declaring to the universe that you are something. If you say that you are not something or the other, you are declaring to the universe that you lack this. You are essentially admitting that you cannot and will not be capable of something. If you believe that something is impossible, it will most likely be true.

Take the example of the four-minute mile. In 1954, Roger Bannister became the first human to run a mile in under four minutes. Until that time, no one had thought it would be possible. Doctors believed that if anyone even tried to do it, they would collapse on the spot because their heart wouldn't be able to take the pressure.

But, Roger Bannister said, "I can, and I will."

On the day of the race in which he attempted to go for the four-minute mile, there were doctors present to ensure that he wouldn't die during his attempt. He crossed the finish line with a time of 3 minutes and 59.4 seconds.

Did he die?

Yes, in 2018 at the age of 88!

The most interesting part of this story is that Bannister's record stood for a grand total of 46 days... 46 days. That goes to show how doing the seemingly impossible opens the floodgates for others to do it as well.

It is all in the mind.

And it starts by you declaring that you can and will do it.

Indeed, the power of the spoken word has tremendous reverberations throughout the universe.

In virtually all of the cultures in the world, the creator of the universe spoke the words that lead to the creation of the world. Regardless of religion, the Supreme Creator spoke the words that brought the world into existence; that brought humans to be.

The spoken word has a magical connection to the universe.

Think about this example.

People who are poor often go around saying, "I don't have any money. I need money."

And, guess what?

They never have any money.

However, if you shift your focus to something like, "I have debts to pay. I will find additional sources of income. I will get more money to pay my bills," you will find that money will come to you.

It is all in the power of the spoken word.

Whatever you want to do, whatever you want to achieve, whatever you want to be, just be speaking the words, you will be well on your way to doing it.

Of course, it is no good if you say the words but sit on the couch watching TV. If you speak the words, really and truly mean them, and then go about the business of achieving your goal, you will do it. You will achieve anything you want. That includes becoming the best version of yourself.

A great way of putting this concept into practice is by having a mantra.

A mantra is something that you say to yourself, and to others, over and over. In fact, mantras become so ingrained in the minds of people that they become automatic thoughts.

For instance, "Where there's a will, there's a way."

This an old proverb that has become cultural in North America. Any time a situation gets tough, folks who are determined to see it through to the end, call upon this mantra. It is an affirmation that whatever is happening, it will be completed, it will be done.

Another such proverb is "When the going gets tough, the tough get going."

Proverbs, quotes and mantras all have the same powerful effect. However, there is one catch: you truly have to believe it. If you just say it for the sake of saying it, then you will be doing yourself a disservice. By stating something which you don't truly feel, which you don't truly believe, you are only cheating yourself.

Of course, there are plenty of unrealistic things that will not happen or may not happen in the time period you expect. For example, you think that you are capable of going to Mars. While that may sound ridiculous, it is something unrealistic at the moment. Eventually, humans will be able to do this, but it just may exceed our lifetime.

The power of your affirmations, the things you say to yourself, the things you say to others, will undoubtedly shape your life. These affirmations will begin to take hold of the reality surrounding you. You will attract people with the right mindset, with the right attitudes and the right qualities.

So, if you are seeking your twin flame, why not try something like, "today is a great day to meet my twin flame."

However you choose to phrase it, please keep it positive. Avoid using negatives such as, "I won't have a bad day today." By saying something like that, you are assuming that today will be a bad day. You can put a positive spin on it by saying, "today will be a great day."

You can even take it up a notch, especially after a terrible day, "today was a bad day, but tomorrow will be a good day." Such affirmations will help you put bad days behind you and move on. By keeping your mind positive, you won't dwell on the mistakes you have made. Even if everything goes terribly wrong, there is always some way of framing everything in a positive light.

Sure, there are things which are scary and can certainly put a damper on your mood. So, here's a simple trick: think about what would be the worst thing that can happen and face it. Face it head on. You will see that there isn't all that much to be afraid. More than likely, things will never get to that point, but it they should, you are mentally and spiritually ready for whatever might come.

Chapter 6: Identifying emotional blockages

"The most beautiful place I've ever been is in your heart."

-- Jennifer White

Living with emotional blockages can seem like a constant uphill battle. Living under such circumstances can make life a lot harder than it has to be. It is not only physically draining, but it can also become mentally exhausting.

That is why we will be taking a look at seven signs which you can use to spot emotional blockages.

In tthis chapter, we will deal with how you can identify the telltale signs that you have been living with this condition.

For some people, it is a sad reality when they realize that they have been living with emotional blockages their entire lives. Most of the time, these blockages emerge in childhood. They progress through adolescence until reaching adulthood. By this time, these blockages are so strong, that they just become the new normal.

Well, there is no doubt that emotional blockages are not normal. As such, there is quite a bit you can do to break free from those negative patterns.

Given the fact that the mind and the body are interconnected, there is no question that whatever is affecting the mind and the spirit, will naturally affect the body. Consequently, there are clear physical signs which you can look out for.

Furthermore, the mental and emotional signs which you exhibit on a daily basis are also a clear indicator of what is happening inside yourself. Please bear in mind that you need look no further than inside your own heart in order to find the answers to your troubles.

Without further ado, let's have a look at the seven signs that you can use to identify emotional blockages.

Sign #1: Constantly feeling down and tired

This sign is the first one because it is the most obvious. A happy person is generally upbeat and cheerful. That is as plain as the light of day. And while it is perfectly normal to end up tuckered out after a long day at work, or even a very tough week, some rest and relaxation will help you get back on track.

Often, recovery means taking some time off to socialize with friends and family, spend time on a hobby, or taking a trip somewhere. Other times, all you really need is just some time to unwind with your favorite TV show or a good book.

However, there are times when you might be subjected to prolonged periods of stress and anxiety. It might be due to a demanding job, a difficult time in your family life, or both. When this occurs, extended periods of constant pressure can lead to burnout.

When normal people burn out, they may experience mild symptoms from sleep deprivation and moodiness, to actual illness such as high blood pressure or even a heart attack.

Barring any tragic outcomes, leaving stress and anxiety untreated can lead to emotional blockages. Such blockages end up leading the individual to suffer from chronic fatigue, that is, the feeling that you can never get enough sleep. When this occurs, it might even be necessary to take medication in order to help deal with hormonal imbalances that may have resulted from a burnout.

If left untreated, burnout can lead to depression. This is the lowest point that a person can hit. This is the point where it seems that all hope is lost and there is nothing left to do but just play out the string. These are people you constantly see in a bad mood. They rarely smile and do not partake in fun activities.

Indeed, physical fatigue and symptoms of depression can completely block you off from any communication with your higher being. It can lead you to live through gray days. Every day seems like a routine. It seems as though there is nothing to live for.

In the event that such feelings arise from a traumatic episode, it is clear that unresolved issues have simply taken over the mind of the individual. They are unable to function properly because the mind has decided to shut down. When this occurs, the body begins to pay for it. The disconnect between the mind, body and spirit can lead the individual to feeling exhausted and sad all the time.

The good news is that liberating the energy in your chakras will help you break through that barrier. When you do, you will feel how you become filled with energy with each passing day. Although, you may also have to make significant changes to your life such as leaving toxic environments and people. Please keep in mind that your mental, physical and emotional health are worth so much more than anything else.

Sign #2: Ignoring issues

This is practically living in denial. This is not accepting the fact that something is bothering you. In fact, this is what essentially happens when you take something and just sweep it under the carpet. You pretend that whatever it was that happened doesn't affect you.

In some cases, you try to put on a brave face in public. You don't want others to see how something is affecting you. You would rather prove yourself to be stoic rather than letting your emotions out, especially in public.

Often times, it is easier to just pretend things never happened and move on with life. The reason for this is because you find that life doesn't allow you to take time off from your work, or perhaps you can't really afford to seek professional help.

However, the problem with pretending that nothing is wrong is that, over time, these issues can fester and become even deeper issues. In a way, it's like leaving a physical ailment which you thought wasn't that bad, but over time, it just got worse and worse.

Indeed, ignoring an issue is asking for trouble. Down the road, you will find that whatever issues you had only got worse. But these issues won't catch up with you until they are way worse than they originally were. When they do catch up to you, you will find that you won't be able to deal with them quite as easily as you could have.

By then, you will be forced to take time off and possibly rack up some medical bills in the process. It will be very hard for you to get back on track simply because more time and effort will be needed and helping you get through the original issue and all of the new issues that arose from the original one.

If something has happened to you, something that has really gotten to you (you can tell when something really gets to you), it is best to take a step back and address as best you can. You may have to burn a sick day. You may have to talk to your boss and ask for help. Or, you might have to rely upon your friends and loved ones to support you through tough times.

Whatever you choose to do, it will be alright. The important thing is to get help when you need it. By ignoring a problem, you will never get the help you need, much less solve the issue. So, please fight through the urge to just suck it up. Ask for help if you need it. When it comes to health issues, there is no sense in trying to be brave.

Sign #3: Trying to be a people-pleaser

This one is really a gray area.

It is one thing to devote your time and energies toward helping others. After all, giving is a great way in which we can dedicate our lives to the greater good. But what happens when you give so much that there isn't any more left to give?

This is a rather common situation for a lot of folks. They give themselves for the benefit of others. They devote their lives to attempting to help those who need it. Indeed, it is an altruistic effort that leads to wonderful outcomes in the lives of those who are in need.

However, there is a situation when you attempt to please everyone. This is hardly feeding the hungry or helping the poor. This is attempting to satisfy others' selfish whims. When this happens, you, as a people pleaser, end up becoming spent and even frustrated because you feel you are not being appreciated for your efforts. You are not getting anything out of your efforts. In fact, you might feel that others are simply taking advantage of you. This not only leads to feeling used, but it leads you to question why you even do things for anybody.

The problem is that you can't stop.

You are convinced that you must keep on doing what others want, otherwise, they won't be in your lives anymore.

Do you think that sounds extreme?

Consider some examples.

Think about the people who work really hard to please their parents. Now, these aren't ordinary parents. These are the parents that push their children to become some kind of superstar performer or athlete. These are the parents who don't really have their child's best interest in mind. Rather, they are trying to live through their children in an attempt to right all of the things that went wrong for them.

The child grows up in this environment where they are being constantly pushed to live up to their parents' expectations. They are not allowed to explore their own personalities. Instead, they are being constantly told what to do. They cannot be free to act for themselves. Everything is dictated to them.

Because of these circumstances, the individual becomes afraid that if they don't go along, their parents won't love them anymore. And yes, there are parents who use emotional blackmail to get their children to go along.

Then, there are folks who go along with everything their social group says for fear that they will be ostracized. These could be friends, classmates or just people in their community. They think a certain way and act a certain way.

They expect others to comply if they want to be a part of that social group. For instance, a shy and socially challenged teenager will do anything they can to become a part of the popular group. They will stoop to whatever low is needed in order to gain acceptance. Over time, the leaders of the social group will demand more and more. Ultimately, the people pleaser will end up spent and feeling humiliated at the things they had to go through in order to gain acceptance.

You might also see such behavior in marriages. This type of scenario goes both ways. You have a husband, or wife, that strives to do everything they can to please their spouse. The problem is that the spouse takes advantage of that and demands more and more. The other spouse feels obliged to comply lest the other leaves them. The risk of being dumped is too great. So, they keep calm and plough through.

Finally, one day it is too much. How that overburdened spouse reacts depends on their personal character. Some folks may just curl up and stop functioning. Others may get physically ill. Others may just explode and act irrationally.

These examples all underscore the toll that attempting to please everyone can take on a person. This is why it is healthy to say "no" on occasion. It's best to commit to the things you can really do and are willing to see through. It is not only a courtesy to others, but it is also a way of keeping your best interests in mind.

Sign #4: Unrealistic expectations

Having lofty aspirations is the hallmark of any successful person. After all, why settle for the moon when you can shoot for the stars?

The problem with that logic is that if you have unrealistic expectations for the people in your life, you will be constantly disappointed. Now, that isn't to say that you should set the bar high. What it does mean is that if you set the bar too high, most folks won't be able to reach the level you want.

This often happens to parents. They expect their children to become overachievers. Then, they realize that their children's talents lie in other fields. Yet, these parents are hellbent on having their children excel in the area they have decided they must become. This leads to constant disappointment by the parents.

Another such example can be seen in romantic relationships. You might enter a relationship expecting to be with the perfect man or woman. You expect them to be everything you could ever possibly need. But when it turns out that they are human and have imperfections, you become disillusioned at the thought of them not being what you expected.

Sure, there are negative traits that are deal breakers. But the fact is that humans are humans. They have flaws and will make mistakes. So, by setting unrealistically high expectations, you are only setting up yourself for failure. You are dooming your relationships with others from the get-go.

Imagine if you met your twin flame today, yet your expectations were so high that you would actually be disappointed by them?

This would end up becoming the worst possible thing you could do to the relationship or your life. Regardless of what kind of relationship it is, you would ruin your one and only twin flame's chance to make you happy.

After all, your twin flame is only out to make you happy… as best they can. You cannot blame them for trying their best to make you happy in spite of their imperfections and flaws. What you can do is help them enter a situation in which they have every chance to succeed. That not only breeds confidence, but it also breeds a mutual understanding that can lead to a prolonged period of happiness and fulfillment.

Sign #5: You can't let go of the past

This topic is so important that we have an entire chapter devoted to it.

For now, it is worth noting that the past is the past. So, why hold on to it?

Sure, there are valuable lessons which the past has taught. Even some of the worst experiences you have lived through have served to teach you something valuable about the universe, and yourself.

However, there are negative experiences which leave an indelible mark on our psyche. There are things, and people, which you just cannot let go. You wish you could, but you are just so attached to them that they won't let you move on. It is like you are stuck in mud and can't accelerate enough to get out.

Indeed, being stuck in a situation such as this can essentially ruin your life. Dwelling on the past can take such strong hold of you that you cannot continue living.

This is very common as a result of break-ups, the death of loved ones, traumatic experiences (such as those lived by war veterans), or simply an event which has marked you for the rest of your life. Breaking through these barriers can be tough. The emotional blockages that can result from such transformational events can leave a person without the will to live.

If you have been through an event, then you can clearly relate. Nevertheless, you have gotten to this point in spite of everything that has happened to you. In deeper and more meaningful ways, you have understood that holding on to the past, however hard it can be to let things go, is only doing you harm.

When you are able to let go, you will be able to transform pain and sorrow into a constructive part of your life. You will be able to provide yourself, and those around you, with the opportunity to share the wonderful things that you have to offer to one another. As such, letting go of the past is not only healthy, but it is also essential in your journey, in your transition, from who you are today, to the best possible version of yourself.

Sign #6: Procrastination

There is always something we are looking to put off, right?

Absolutely. There is always something we are looking to avoid or leave for another day. However, when make a habit of leaving things for another day, it might be a sign of deeper trouble. It might be an indicator that there is something that we are looking to avoid altogether.

Perhaps it is something that you are running away from. Or perhaps it is something that you think is coming after you, but you can't stand to face it. Naturally, we are all afraid of uncertainty and the unknown. We are all concerned about the future and what it may hold. But when we purposely begin putting things off as much as we can, it is like we're trying to avoid responsibility for the things in our lives.

In the majority of cases, extreme procrastination is just that, putting things off because we are looking to avoid the responsibility that comes with many of the facets in life. You start to look at the circumstances of your life as a burden. That, in itself, can be overwhelming. As a result, you begin to neglect the things which you should be paying attention to in favor of other things which don't necessarily provide you with productive outcomes.

If anything, procrastination, can just be a way of eluding those things which are causing you harm. Think about being in a toxic work environment. Naturally, you would like to avoid anything work-related as much as possible.

What if your family life is causing you harm? You would try your best to avoid such situations.

While hard, it is best to face things head on. It can be overwhelming to think that you would have to face some of these situations. But the fact of the matter is that taking responsibility of the circumstances in your life is more than just assuming a role, it is about empowerment. When you are empowered, you are certain that you are the only one that has power over the situations in your life. So, don't be afraid to take the bull by the horns.

When you become fully empowered, you will begin to see just how great your life can be. All you would need to do is try your best to become the best version of yourself. The rest will come with time. So, don't be afraid of stepping up. You will do just fine.

Sign #7: Unhealthy habits

This one takes the cake.

When you are emotionally distressed, particularly in times of great anguish and sorrow, it is very common to turn to substances which can help you ease the pain that you feel. For some, overeating becomes a coping mechanism. This might include binges on sweets or junk food.

For others, substance abuse such as alcohol, drugs and cigarettes can become the ideal coping mechanism. The fact of the matter is that when you load up on these substances, you are only further intoxicating your body. This intoxication leads to a clogging of all of your body's natural mechanisms. The end result is your body's impaired functioning.

This impairment will consequently lead you to lose touch with your higher being. Of course, it's fun to go out on a Friday night after a tough week at work and have a few drinks. But when it becomes far too habitual, then you might have a problem in your hands.

In today's modern society, reliance on substances or medication as a means of coping with daily issues has become commonplace. Healthy individuals try to find the best possible way to process their feelings. This could include exercise, yoga, meditation and other such activities. Having a healthy social life is important. In addition, counting on friends in times of distress is an absolute must.

If you find yourself using some of these substances a little more than you should, you might want to consider cutting back on them, if not, cutting them out altogether. Substances, even with the occasional use of recreational drugs, can lead your mind-body connection to go out of whack. Thus, you may end up losing touch with your higher being. Needless to say, that is hardly conducive to pinpointing your twin flame.

One final consideration

Emotional blockages can certainly be tough to spot. By taking the time to do some introspection, that is, to think about who you are, why you do things that you do, and where you want to go with your life, will go a long way toward putting yourself on the road to wholeness. You will be able to see who you really are and what you want to get out of life. When you are able to see this in yourself, you will begin to gain a perspective on life that no one can ever show you.

This will most assuredly reveal the path to your twin flame.

Chapter 7: Dealing with emotional blockage

"If you are not more alive when in love then you my friend are in love with the wrong one."

-- Nikki Rowe

Wholeness is one of the prerequisites to enjoying a fulfilling twin flame relationship. If you are not whole and at peace with yourself, you cannot truly expect to find that happiness and joy that comes with being with the one you have been searching for all your life.

In fact, you may find that the relationship you had been craving for all your life will wither away simply because you weren't ready for it.

Indeed, being ready for a twin flame relationship requires quite a bit of preparation. A twin flame relationship is like finally making it to the major leagues. All of a sudden you are at the big show. You are with the big team. The time for games is over. It is now time you show your partner how much you care for them and how much you are prepared to give them.

This is why finding that place in yourself takes a lot of soul searching. It takes a great deal of understanding and acceptance. Yes, finding that place takes some time, but it is something that only you can do.

If only there were some pill you could take… some magic concoction. Alas, there is none. Just some good, old-fashioned elbow grease. This will undoubtedly help you achieve the state of oneness that can allow you to be the one that your twin flame expects you to be.

However, some, if not most of us, have to deal with emotional blockages. These blockages are simply repressed emotions that are shoved down into the deepest parts of our soul. We are talking about both good and bad emotions. The kind of emotions that are associated with fulfillment, or dejection. We are talking about a spectrum of emotions that can lead you to essentially lose your mind if not tended to properly.

Emotional blockages come in all shapes and sizes. They can be the product of years and years of abuse and neglect, prolonged periods of stress and anxiety, or they can be traced back to a single, traumatic event that can even destroy lives.

These emotional blockages are the psyche's natural response to trauma that may occur at various points in an individual's life. When these traumas occur, the mind has two options: deal with it or sweep it under the rug.

Depending on the circumstances of an individual, they can deal with it and go through the healing process, or they can just forget about it and move on.

On the surface, "getting over" a traumatic event and moving on can become a stopgap measure. But over time, it will invariably come back to bite the individual. You cannot expect things to simply go away on their own.

Look at it in these terms:

You are out running on a sunny morning. You are taking advantage of the weather to get a good run in. Suddenly, you miss seeing a rock and trip. You fall and scrape your knee. At this point, you have two options: you either call for help and sit there until someone helps you, or you get up and keep moving. Perhaps you can "walk it off" until it feels better.

Conventional wisdom would consider this injury to be a minor one. So, it shouldn't cause you to miss any time from work or alter your lifestyle significantly. If anything, you might be uncomfortable for a few days. Mostly likely, you'll just have to deal with the pain while your scrapes and cuts heal. Even when your injuries heal, you may be left with a tiny reminder of your spill in the form of a scar.

In emotional terms, such circumstances tend to be treated the same. If you have a minor incident that creates emotional cuts and scrapes, you are expected to "walk it off" and get on with your life. And sure enough, most of the time, minor incidents go away after a few days. The only sign that may be left of that negative incident may be a bad memory.

Now, imagine the same example of running in the park, except this time you break your ankle. You immediately feel that there is something seriously wrong with your ankle. You know that this isn't just some cuts and scrapes. This is much more serious. So, you call for help, perhaps a friend, or even paramedics, you are taken to the hospital and x-rays confirm that you have a broken ankle.

At that point, would you expect that the doctor would tell you to walk it off?

Do you believe the doctor would tell you to forget about your problem because it'll heal on its own?

Sure, your broken ankle will eventually heal on its own. Nevertheless, the bone will not set correctly, and you'll end up with a physical limitation due to the fracture not healing properly.

On a physical level, it is perfectly clear how a physical injury is absolutely detrimental to your body's overall health and wellbeing. After all, no one would ignore a broken bone. Of course, you could technically just plough through, but why would you put yourself through needless pain and anguish?

So, why are we expected to suck it up and power through when we have emotional distress?

Why aren't we afforded the same consideration when we have the emotional equivalent of a broken bone?

The fact is that often times, emotional distress isn't taken as seriously as physical distress simply because it isn't quite as evident as a physical injury. A broken ankle is rather obvious. But a broken heart isn't quite as obvious.

Consider this situation:

A loved one has passed away. You have gotten news that this dear and beloved person has passed on after a prolonged illness. You have to go through the traumatic experience of the illness and then the sorrow and grief of this person's passing.

Given the closeness of your relationship you are deeply affected. You are in shock and in disbelief that this person has finally left. You are at a loss for words. You simply cannot function properly.

How much time do you think you would be able to take off from work?

Do you think your company would give you all the time off you needed until you got better?

Do you think your friends and family would support you the same way as if you had broken your ankle?

Is there a parking space for the emotionally challenged?

The fact is that our society doesn't hold emotional distress in the same regard as it does physical injury. It seems that because physical injuries are so obvious, we tend to pay greater attention to them. However, with emotional injuries, we tend to ignore them since we can't really see them. But we can feel them alright.

As a matter of fact, emotional injuries tend to feel just as bad, or even worse, than physical injuries. So, the pain is there, it's just that we can't really see where it is coming from.

Origin of emotional trauma and distress

When discussing physical trauma and distress, the question that usually comes up is: how does it form? That is, where does it come from?

The answer to that has several layers.

Most emotional blockage stems from some type of emotional trauma that overwhelms the psyche. When this occurs, the individual needs to find a way to deal with the pain and anguish that comes from the trauma. The easiest way to deal with it is to shut things off.

What does that mean?

It means that when the feelings associated to a traumatic event, or a succession of events, become too much, the individual will just shut off. They will disconnect from their feelings in such a way that they no longer feel what's going on. They just "log off," in a manner of speaking.

Shutting off feelings as a response to emotional distress is similar to taking a large dose of painkillers in order to get away from feeling a massive physical injury; it does nothing to actually fix the injury, but at least it makes the pain go away.

Emotional blockages may arise from one, singular event, that causes an individual's psyche to become overwhelmed. Think about events such as accidents, the death of a loved one, or being a victim of a terrible act. These singular events can have such a profound effect on the individual, that they are unable to cope with them.

In most cases, they will require some type of psychological therapy. This generally helps most individuals as they begin to understand the effect that the event had on them. In general, therapy is enough to help them get through the experience and find a way back to a sense of normalcy. However, there are many other folks who go through such events and never get the treatment they need.

In those cases, the initial shock wears off over time. This leads them to believe they have "gotten over" the problem. But the injury is still there. This emotional injury may heal on its own. This can happen especially if you have the ability to self-heal through meditation and introspection. However, there are cases when the individual is simply unable to cope with the problem. So, it gets locked away, that is, compartmentalized somewhere, hopefully, never to be heard from again.

Another source for trauma is the prolonged exposure to a stressful situation and/or environment. There are times when an individual is exposed to a situation in which they are under continuously stressful situations or in a toxic environment. As such, they are not influenced by a single event that will essentially ruin their lives. Rather, they are subject to a constant stream of stress, anxiety and even abuse. When this happens, trauma is built up over time.

However, there comes a point where the person is simply unable to deal with the feelings that get built up. Even if those feelings are compartmentalized, the individual needs to blow off steam at some point. When that happens, any type of reaction from such individuals is possible.

Consider this situation:

You have a toxic environment at work. Your boss is hardly the nicest person in the world. You have a terrible commute, the pay is lousy, you constantly work overtime and your job is rather demanding. Your colleagues are no help as they are just as bummed out as you are.

Since you don't have much time for anything, you don't do exercise, you don't have a healthy and nutritious diet, and you tend to watch television quite a bit. You are glued to your phone most of the time. Your social life isn't that great, either.

While this situation is hardly a traumatic event of epic proportions, it helps build up negative energy over time. As it builds up, there is a constant influx of negative energy that cannot be ignored. Even if you just ignore it and move on, there will come a point when it will be simply too much to handle.

This is where an emotional blockage can simply cause a person to shut down.

Have you ever seen people that just look like automatons? They just seem like they are on auto-pilot and don't really seem to be aware of what they are doing?

To folks who have emotional blockages, life is just one big shade of gray. They aren't worried or concerned about engaging the marvel of life. They are just concerned about getting through the month. They are only concerned about the next paycheck and paying the bills.

The problem with emotional blockages

When you put an emotional blockage into perspective, you are cutting yourself off from the more subtle aspects of your being. Your emotional blockages essentially sever the lines of communication between you and your spiritual being.

When you cut yourself off from the more subtle aspect of your being, then you are also cutting yourself off from that spiritual connection with your twin flame. Even if you are totally ready for your twin flame reunion, you won't be able to recognize them. You could have that wonderful person sitting next to you, and you wouldn't be able to tell the difference.

Earlier in this book, we talked about how your heart is the best tool which you can use to determine who your twin flame is. There are no magic formulas or spells which can make your twin flame appear. And even if there were, you still must be emotionally available for them. Otherwise, the connection, the link, between twin flames may never occur.

There have been cases when twin flames meet at one point in their lives, but one simply isn't emotionally ready for the meeting. This causes the flames to run away from the situation. This leads to a "runner" and "chaser" effect.

When you are not emotionally ready for your twin flame, the intensity of your relationship will cause you to bail. Often, the emotional rollercoaster that it is a twin flame relationship proves to be too much for the one who is emotionally unready or unavailable. That leads them to feel overwhelmed.

Then, you hear classic lines, such as those in the movies, "I am just not ready for a commitment," "this is all moving too fast," or "I need some space."

Yes, some of those lines can be pretty lame excuses. But they do hold a kernel of truth.

In twin flame relationships (assuming they are romantic), the emotionally unavailable half will try to find a way to cope with the intense feelings. Since they have been emotionally disconnected, the rush of emotions triggers a panic reaction in their mind.

In cases when the twin flame is not romantic, flames simply miss their chance. They are unable to recognize that this other person is the real deal. So, they push them away, they run away, or they simply ignore them.

When this happens, the odds of your twin flame coming back into your life are null unless you are able to remove the emotional blockages holding your back. When you do, then you might find that the person you least expected was actually your twin flame.

In other cases, the removal of those blockages sends a spiritual beacon to your twin flame that you are ready for them. It is like an old Buddhist proverb, "the teacher appears when the student is ready."

How to deal with emotional blockages

The approach to dealing with emotional blockages is twofold.

First of all, you need to understand why you have this emotional blockage in the first place. Perhaps you may not be able to narrow it down to the exact time and date of its occurrence, but you will be able to understand why it's there.

Secondly, you need to liberate your energy which is trapped inside. This can be done through a combination of meditation, introspection and forgiveness.

Often, the first, and most significant step toward healing your emotional blockage is by admitting that it is there. Granted, there are people who will never admit it. But by listening to this message, you are listening to the call of your higher being. So, if there is a blockage within you, it has given way just enough for you to realize that there is a higher being calling you.

When you recognize that there might be a blockage which is affecting you, you can choose to seek help. This can be in the form of a trusted therapist who can listen and offer support, or by trusting your feelings to a very good friend or relative. Just by having someone you can confide in will enable you to let those feelings out.

Often, letting those feelings out can lead to some explosive reactions. You might recall memories that have been repressed for years. Or, you might relive traumatic events. When that happens, you feel vulnerable. This sense of vulnerability can become too much for some to handle.

It is important to have someone you can rely on for emotional support. They can help you by being a shoulder to lean on or a friendly helping hand. As you begin to open up, you will begin to reconnect with your emotions. That emotional reconnection is essential in your journey.

As you begin to reconnect, you are opening the door to your twin flame. The signals that your twin flame is broadcasting in your direction will now become evident. You will be able to pick up on what they are trying to tell you. That may very well lead you to your reunion.

If your twin flame is sitting right there, next to you, you will be able to recognize who they are. If you still haven't found them, your radar will now be active. This will surely make it a lot easier for both of you to reunite.

Please bear in mind that healing emotional blockages can take some time and it is often a painful process. But there are times when a little pain is needed in order to clear your mind and your soul of toxic elements. This will also lead you to seek out environments that will be less detrimental to your spiritual self.

The other important aspect to releasing yourself from emotional blockages is to connect with your higher being. This is something which can't be done on the therapist's couch. This is something that you need to work on by yourself. This is a process that only you and your higher being can work on.

The most effective way of achieving this is through meditation.

If you have practiced meditation before, then you are familiar with how it works.

Please keep in mind that one of the most common mistakes made in meditation is to work hard at clearing the mind. Mediation is not so much about clearing your mind as it is about listening to your thoughts. Focus on the thoughts racing through your mind.

What are they?

What are they telling you?

Can you understand why you are thinking the thoughts that you have?

Take the time to pay attention to those thoughts. Take the time to analyze why they are there in the first place. Perhaps they aren't even yours. Perhaps someone else has put them there.

Then, decide that those thoughts which are causing you stress and anxiety must go. They can no longer stay inside of you. As you gradually visualize them disappearing from your life, you will begin to shift from feelings of anxiety and even depression, to feelings of calm and peace of mind.

Of course, if at any time thoughts of harming yourself become too frequent or overwhelming, please get in touch with a trusted therapist, your loved ones, friends, or anyone who can help you. There might be a situation in which the rush of feelings may lead you to have strong thoughts and feelings related to harming yourself. So, the last thing that you want to be is alone. Please keep in mind that there are people out there who want you and need you in their lives even if they aren't your twin flame.

One of the most important things you can do to help you connect with your higher being is through the liberation of your chakras. The chakras generally become clogged up over time even if you don't have any emotional blockages.

Your chakras are points of concentration in your energy. These points all have their specific functions and they can all become blocked due to negative feelings. Other times, they just need a little cleaning up.

This is an overview of what each chakra does:

The crown chakra is located at the top of your head. It is considered to be the pathway to your highest spiritual being. Emotional blockages can completely cut off connection with your higher being.

The third eye chakra is located right between your eyes, slightly above your eyebrows. It is where the individual begins to awaken, hence, opening eyes when waking after sleep. So, if you have a blockage, your third eye will close.

The throat chakra is located right on the throat where the vocal chords would be. This chakra is associated with the voice of creation. If you do not let your feelings out, your voice will essentially become mute.

The heart chakra is located at the center of your chest. This chakra is generally associate with feelings, with the union of male and female. Thus, the perception of the heart producing feelings come from this chakra. Emotional blockages essentially damage this chakra and close it off.

The solar plexus chakra can be found in the navel area. This is considered to be the self-discovery chakra. If your balance is out of whack, it could lead to your "losing you way."

The sacral chakra is located in the genital area. It is the sexual chakra. This is considered to be the chakra of creation as it is associated with reproduction. Its blockage can lead to a disconnect of a sexual union.

The root chakra can be found at the base of the spine in the coccygeal region. This is the root of all spiritual self-discovery.

As you can see, each chakra has a very specific function. If one, or all, are blocked, then there is a disconnect between the physical and spiritual body.

With this simple, but effective meditation exercise, you can visualize your chakras back into action.

As with the previous meditation and visualization exercises, find a quiet place to sit, or lie flat on your back. Try to avoid relaxation music or sounds as these can become distracting after a while. Now, visualize these seven points throughout your body. Imagine each point lighting up. As each point lights up, visualize it as a spinning disc whose light grows stronger and stronger.

You can choose to focus on individual chakras, concentrating on the its color, shape and size. You can also visualize all chakras lighting up, spinning at the same time, in unison, at the same speed and with the same intensity.

This visualization exercise can help you begin to liberate the energy that has been blocked and/or built up in each chakra. As you gain more and more practice with this exercise, you will begin to feel a tingling sensation in the area where each chakra is located. In addition, you might feel the same sensation throughout the day.

The ultimate goal of this exercise is to allow your higher being to communicate with your earthly consciousness. Over time, you will feel more subtle, lighter and simply more in tune with your own feelings.

Eventually, unblocking the energy in your chakras will allow you to become more receptive to the potential reunion with your twin flame. Ultimately, when the reunion happens, you will be in synch. You will be ready to reunite with your twin flame, regardless of the type of relationship you are meant to have and move on to the next level in your life's mission.

Chapter 8: Breaking free of those blockages

"We think we meet someone with our eyes, but we actually meet them with our soul."

-- Mimi Novic

In the previous chapter, we focused on the warning signs of an emotional blockage. As such, the first step to improving this aspect of your life is identifying the blockage.

That is why this chapter will focus on ways in which you can break free from the blockages affecting your life and your health.

The road to breaking free from emotional blockages has several twists and turns that will lead you to a unique journey. You may have companions along the way, but the journey itself is yours alone. Therefore, you need to make your best effort in turning your ship around.

In addition, breaking free from emotional blockages requires consistency and commitment on your part. You cannot expect to work on yourself here and there and expect wonderful results. The road to becoming the best version of yourself is completed one step at a time.

That being said, this chapter intends to provide you some tips and strategies that can help you make the most of this journey. These tips and strategies can serve as signposts on the road. While you are the one who holds the roadmap, having directions and pointers can certainly help make the journey a lot easier.

So, let's take a deeper a look at some great ways in which you can get started on your personal journey to achieving the best version of yourself.

Strategy #1: Live in the moment

Given the pace of modern life, it is very easy to get lost in the shuffle. The amount of distractors that we encounter on a daily basis is enormous. Having a smartphone alone is enough to keep you constantly distracted. The incessant pinging and buzzing of our phones can even lead us to feel stress and anxiety on a seemingly permanent basis.

Furthermore, we tend to get caught up in the past and in the future. We dwell on the events of the past and fear the events of the future. The problem is that neither the past nor the future exist. The past is lost in the past, and the future hasn't arrived yet.

As such, worrying about the past or the future can only lead to needless stress and anxiety. After all, why torture yourself over something which you cannot change? And, why mortify yourself over something which you can control?

This is why living in the present is one of the most important things you can do to help liberate yourself from emotional blockages. When you let go of the past, you are freeing yourself from the shackles of events that have held you back.

While it is not easy to let go of the past, reliving painful and even traumatic events is useless unless you plan to do something about it.

For instance, if you lived through a painful experience, say, the loss of a loved one, you can do something about it. You can choose to let go of the painful memories and uncover the true reason why you feel the way you do.

Perhaps you are feeling guilty over something you did not do or say.

Perhaps you are feeling overwhelmed by feelings of abandonment.

Perhaps you are feeling fearful of losing someone else.

Whatever the case, holding on to the past will only rub salt in the wound over and over.

If you are concerned or fearful about the future, you are opening the door to useless suffering over something that may not even happen.

Consider this:

You are fearful and concerned over losing your job. You feel that your job stability is in jeopardy. Consequently, you are suffering over something that might just be in your mind.

However, if you live in the present, you are in control of the situation. You are in control over what happens at work today. You are in control over your actions in your place of work. After all, there is not much you can control beyond what you do. You cannot control what others do no matter how hard you try. If you do end up losing your job, it won't be because you didn't give it your all.

So, that begs the question: what happens if you do actually love your job?

This is something which you need to be prepared for. You can make preparations and contingency plans, but in the end, it is your mindset that will help you get through whatever comes.

By living in the present, you can focus on what is in front you, what you have at hand. These are things which you can control. You can perfectly mold the present to suit your needs. While some things are not quite so simple to change, you have the power to make choices which can alter the future in such a way that you can create the circumstances that you want.

When you take charge of the present, your mind is constantly working on building the future that you want. What more could you ask for?

Do you recall the importance of taking responsibility for your actions? This is what empowerment is all about.

Of course, you can and will make mistakes. But the mistakes that you make will serve as learning experiences which can help you grow into the role you have envisioned for yourself. Your ability to take control of your actions reduces the amount of stress you will feel. It will also help you find stability and certainty especially if your life is filled with turmoil and conflict.

Think about it.

Imagine you are in the middle of chaos, yet you know exactly where to go. While others may be running around, clueless and distraught, you actually know what to do. This type of power is not reserved to uber-talented people. It can be achieved by anyone who knows what they want and where they want to go.

Thus, living in the present will become one of your biggest tools in improving your outlook on life.

Strategy #2: Listen to your body

Often, we don't pay nearly as much attention as we should to the signals our body gives us.

When we fail to pay attention to the clues our body is giving us, we fail to maximize the communication between all aspects of our being. Naturally, we react when we have a headache or digestive distress. But we generally fail to react when we feel a knot in our stomach or perhaps a lump in our throat.

The fact of the matter is that your body and your spiritual being are in constant communication. They signal each other back in forth throughout the day. When you are able to pick up on those signs, then you quickly learn to identify the emotions that come with such physical manifestations.

For example, you might feel a sharp pain in your chest (no, hopefully it is not a heart attack) every time anyone mentioned a loved one who has parted or triggers a memory from a terrible incident.

As you become aware of the signs your body gives you, you will be able to catch these negative feelings in the act. When you are able to pick up on these clues on a consistent basis, you are then able to stop and analyze your feelings. You can ask yourself why you are feeling the way you. You can judge why you react the way you do.

One positive way to help you catch yourself in certain behaviors or certain reactions is by going on the buddy system. You can ask a friend, family member or even a colleague to point out every time you react, or act, in a certain way.

For instance, you can ask a colleague to point out every time you get upset. The purpose of doing this is not to highlight the problem, but rather to help you pinpoint the triggers which lead you to act in this manner. That way, you can identify the situations which lead you to become angry or upset. Moreover, you can do something about it.

If you find that you are constantly becoming upset over the comments and behavior of your coworkers, it might be time to pull yourself away from the negative situation which is causing you to feel affected. Perhaps you might even ask for a transfer to another department. In the worst of cases, you may need to find another job.

Of course, this example might seem a bit extreme, but it serves to illustrate how you can purposely identify the triggers which are causing you to feel down, upset, angry, or any other negative feeling which is harming you.

Also, becoming aware of your feelings, at the moment they begin to creep up on you, is a way of living in the present. In doing so, you are taking your attention away from the past or the future, and you are focusing on what is happening here and now.

The biggest benefit that you will begin to see when you live in the here and now, is that you will slowly begin to break away from negative patterns. As you break away from these negative patterns, you will then begin to pull yourself away from the triggers which cause you to feel like this. In addition, you will be able to confront those triggers as you are now clear what they are.

Strategy #3: Confront the issue

When you become familiar with the triggers that lead to your emotional reactions, or lack thereof, you will arrive at a point where you can confront the issues that are affecting you.

There are times when the issues are not quite as difficult. Then, there are times when issues are so serious that you can't go at it alone.

Let's consider some examples.

Imagine you are in a toxic workplace environment in which there is one co-worker that is making it exceptionally hard for you to get along well. You have decided to stand your ground as you need the job and do not plan to leave. Since you have identified this toxic co-worker as the cause for your negative feelings, you have decided to confront this person about the issue.

By facing the issue head on, you are able to determine where the root cause lies. Perhaps this person is so insecure that they need to attack others in order to feel better about themselves. Whatever the case, addressing the root cause will help you move away from the emotional blockage that can result from such a negative situation.

However, there are cases when the underlying cause of an emotional blockage isn't quite so simple. In such cases, you might need to seek professional help. By seeking out professional help, you can work together to find the root causes of such emotional blockages.

There are times when uncovering these blockages takes time and effort. Sometimes, it isn't as simple as having traditional therapy. There are times when other methods need to be used such as hypnosis.

Under hypnosis, a qualified professional can take you through the various steps of your life in order for you to relive events which have been potentially traumatic. This professional can assist you in identifying such events so that the underlying cause can be revealed.

Nevertheless, it is important to have adequate accompaniment during such a journey as the revelation of events may be too much to handle. When this occurs, the last thing you want is to be alone.

Think about it.

You are going to relive one of the worst, if not, the worst experience of your life. Do you really want to be alone for that?

The fact of the matter is that facing your demons can be a challenging experience, it can be painful, but it can certainly help you get over your blockages once and for all.

That is why you see folks returning to the scene of their most difficult moments. Just by being in the same place where the event took place is enough to help them begin to heal. Other times, they need to see the person who harmed them. By seeing and talking to this person, the healing process can begin.

Then, there are times when you just need to forgive yourself. Whatever happened, more than likely, was not your fault. Perhaps it was no one's fault. That is why you cannot beat yourself up over it. You cannot continue to blame yourself in the hopes of finding some sort of way to make sense of everything that happened.

Furthermore, if there is someone looking to ask for your forgiveness, give them the opportunity to be forgiven. By forgiving someone who has wronged you, you can let go of the pain and find closure. Sure, it won't change what happened in the least bit, but at least you can find closure. Then, the real healing can begin.

Of course, there are times when you cannot see or talk to the person who harmed you. Nevertheless, you can still forgive them. You can make a declaration to the universe that you have forgiven the person, or people, who have harmed you. While you may never forget what they did to you, you will give them the opportunity to be pardoned.

It might be that they won't ever appreciate what you are doing for them. But in the end, you will be better off by giving yourself the chance to let go and move on with the next step in your life.

Strategy #4: Breathing and visualization

Blockages are just that: blockages. They are funnels or bottlenecks in which your feelings and emotions get trapped. They can't pass through properly or they simply get stuck. When that happens, you will find all sorts of emotions getting built up.

As your emotions build up, you will find the pressure increasing more and more. Finally, there comes a point in which the pressure has built up so much that you blow. That reaction can be as violent or as quiet as you can imagine.

There have been cases in which frustrated people lash out with tragic consequences. Then, there are others who quietly get so down on themselves that they even decide to take their own lives without saying a word.

However, here is a good strategy that can help you begin to break through those blockages.

It is a combination of visualization and breathing.

When you feel anxiety building up. When you feel negative thoughts creeping on you. When you feel the pressure beginning to grow inside, you need to take time out.

If possible, go outside to get some fresh air. Sit down under a tree or neat plants. Close your eyes and take deep breaths. As you breathe, try to visualize your feelings running all across your body. Try to visualize them as a wave that ripples throughout your body.

When the ripples reach your fingertips and your toes, imagine how those feelings dissipate and get lost in the wind. As you breathe, inhale until your lungs are filled to capacity. Then, hold your breath slightly. One or two seconds will be enough to get the oxygen flowing through your blood and into your brain. As you exhale, do so slowly. You are not sprinting to the finish line. So, breathe in and breathe our slowly.

If you are at work and unable to leave your place, you can just close your eyes right there and breathe. Just a couple of deep breaths can be enough for you to stop the feeling from advancing. If you are able to lean back into your chair and close your eyes, then do so.

Often, it pays to take five minutes out of your work day to regain your composure. Otherwise, you will be attempting to trudge through the day. However, with such feelings bearing down upon you, you will not be able to fully concentrate on your tasks. Thus, it is essential that you stop negative feelings in their tracks.

One additional benefit of this breathing technique is that it allows you to live in the present. Since you are constantly monitoring your feelings, you are not focused on the past or the future. You are focused on the tasks which you have at hand. Then, if you should feel these emotions coming on, you can take a step back and address them before they get the better of you.

If you have experienced depression in any way, using breathing and visualization techniques can help you find a proper balance between in your overall mood. Of course, depression is not to be taken lightly. Yet, visualization as a tool for getting rid of the blocks is essential in helping you get through difficult spots.

Strategy #5: Make a declaration

As with visualization, you can use the power of words to break through blockages and negative emotions.

You can start your day by declaring what will happen, what you will do and how things are going to turn out. Your declarations to the universe are a singular statement that you are in control of what is happening. You are not a victim of circumstance. You have the power to choose what you will do, how it will be done and even when it will happen.

Naturally, there are many things which we cannot control. Nevertheless, your declarations are a way of making things happen.

For example, if you are in financial distress and need money to get through the month, you can stop anxiety in its tracks and declare that you will find the means to provide the money you need to take care of yourself and your family.

You can make a statement such as, "I can provide everything my family needs." This is a powerful statement that signals to the universe you are not going to take things lying down. You are determined to go out there and make the best of your day.

If you are going through a difficult emotional situation, you can make a declaration such as, "I am better than any of these emotions."

The only catch is that you need to say these things out loud. You actually need to use your voice to say. Of course, it is very powerful to think them. But by actually saying such things, you are ordering the universe to comply.

Yes, we have that power.

Yes, we have the opportunity to mold circumstances to our favor.

You have that power residing in you.

Sure, you don't have to go around yelling at the top of your lungs. But just a firm declaration, as often as possible, is enough to get the ball rolling. The universe will comply and willingly help you achieve what you want.

So, write down your positive affirmations. Write down the thoughts and ideas that will help you get through those blockages. Whatever they are, you can break through them by using the power of your words.

Say your affirmations when you get up in the morning. On the way to work, at the gym, at school, in the showers, well, everywhere. And you will see that soon enough, the tide will begin to turn. There is no question about it.

One final thought

Please bear in mind that emotional blockages take a long time to form. Consequently, they also take some time to break down. You can't really expect to break them overnight. Yet, the decision to break through them is instantaneous. The decision to make a change happens in a single moment.

The work that goes along with breaking through those blockages can be more or less intense. Yet, the need for work is there. Consider this portion of your life as a "work in progress." You can even attach a working title to it. Something like, "on the road to the best version of myself" can become a marker for the end state that you are looking to achieve.

As you begin to break through those blockages, you will find that your quality of life will begin to improve. You will see improvements in your health, in your self-esteem and even in the way others see you.

That alone is enough to help your twin flame reconnect with you.

Chapter 9: Attachment in your life is holding you back

"Some souls just understand each other upon meeting."

-- N.R. Hart

In this chapter, we are going to be taking a look at one of the most important topics in this book.

Attachment is one of the most complex issues that might be holding you back on your journey toward finding your twin flame.

Being attached to something, or someone, is like carrying around a huge weight on your shoulders. It can feel like having a boulder strapped to your neck or even a ton of bricks tied to your feet. No matter how hard you try to swim, the weight keeps pulling you down under water.

If you have ever felt like this, chances are you are being bogged down by an enormous weight which will not let you keep your head above water. What's worse, you may not even realize it's there!

Yes, it is quite common for us to go through life without realizing that there are burdens which are artificially keeping us down. Even when you try your best to keep going, you can't seem to make any headway.

That is why we are going to focus on identifying attachment in such a way that you can understand the various types of attachment and how they play a role in your life. Also, this can allow you to begin finding a starting point on your road to freeing yourself from the chains that are holding you back.

What is attachment?

Attachment is the bond that an individual forms with the people, places and objects around them.

You see examples of this all the time. Most assuredly you have a great number of bonds in your life. The key to this discussion is: what type of bond do you have with the people and things in your life.

For example, what type of bond do you have with the people in your life?

Do you constantly find yourself trying to control or micromanage the relationships you have with others?

Are you a jealous or possessive person?

Perhaps the opposite, you could care less about what happens to those around you.

These types of bonds are a reflection of your particular attachment style. Based on your personal style, you will form bonds which will be healthy or unhealthy to a varying degree. It is these bonds which could affect your life in a negative or positive way.

Healthy bonds can offer you great joy and happiness. Unhealthy bonds can eat away at you slowly until you are totally consumed. This is the basis for unhealthy and even destructive relationships.

In fact, attachments can be so strong that people in destructive, abusive and unhealthy relationships cannot muster up the courage to leave their abuser. It happens all the time and in a varying array of dynamics.

For instance, you have an abusive spouse who constantly exerts abuse and punishment on the other spouse. Yet, the victim is unable to leave because they are afraid of losing them. This type of attachment is so unhealthy that the victim feels a sense of "normalcy" in this type of dynamic.

Then, you have abusive parents who take out their frustration and ill feelings on their children. Their children, even in adulthood, become so attached to the dysfunctional dynamic that they are afraid of leaving their parents for fear of altering their flawed perception of normal. This perpetuates the unhealthy attachment to a point where the victims are completely consumed.

On the other hand, healthy bonds are the hallmark of great friendships, marvelous marriages and harmonious working relationships. However, this isn't something which you can automatically adjust like a thermostat. These types of relationships take time to form. But when they do, they can last a lifetime.

Your relationship, your dynamic with your twin flame, will be filtered by your attachment style. If you allow a negative attachment style take hold of your life, you will enter your twin flame relationship under the mindset. Needless to say, it will undermine your twin flame's chances of building a healthy and loving relationship with you.

As such, it is important to understand the different attachment styles. In identifying your own style, you will be able to get a better grip on your personal dynamic and being to develop the right habits which will ultimately help you achieve happiness and joy with your twin flame.

Attachment styles

Attachment styles have their root in childhood. They are the result of experiences lived during this phase in our lives. As such, they mark our personality for the remainder of our adult experience. Mainly, attachment styles stem from the type of dynamic we have within our family. In this case, the way the child is treated and cared for will determine how well-adjusted the grown individual will become.

Consequently, a child who has a healthy relationship with their parents will end up becoming secure and confident in adulthood. This child will be able to develop the type of relationships which are based on trust and understanding. In general, healthy relationships between parents and children stem from parents being there as much as possible for their children. As such, children are able to rely on their parents for support when they truly need it. Hence, these children are able to fend for themselves much better given their overall sense of security.

When children are the subject of neglect, or simply come from a dysfunctional home, they tend to develop attachment issues in adulthood. These issues may manifest themselves in the inability to develop healthy relationships both on a romantic and social level. As such, these attachment issues become evident in the way they relate to others.

For instance, you might have an individual who is unable to develop strong bonds and relationships with others since they are fearful of rejection and abandonment. These feelings only get stronger as they get older and attempt to engage in much more meaningful relationships. This is why you often see adults who are unable to commit to a long-term relationship.

Nevertheless, improving these issues is possible should you happen to experience any of the negative attachment styles. First of all, it is important to identify them in such a way that you can honestly determine if you are falling under this category.

So, let's take a look at these attachment styles in greater detail.

Secure attachment

Under this attachment style, the individual is a secure person who is able to relate to other people in a healthy and safe manner. Their relationships are based mainly on trust and understanding. Consequently, they are not focused on the possibility of being hurt or somehow affected in a negative manner. Rather, adults who have developed secure attachment relationships can focus on core values such as honesty, independence and emotional connections. Such connections can often last a long time as they are rooted in genuine companionship. In terms of romantic relationships, they are characterized by a sense of understanding, love and collaboration. Indeed, these are the types of relationships which we all strive to develop.

Dismissive avoidant attachment

This attachment style is characterized by the way in which adults attempt to keep their distance at all times. They avoid close contact with other individuals. In fact, you will find that they avoid developing any kind of close bond with any other person, mainly out of fear. However, their relationships are not based on fear, rather, they are mainly based on the suspicion of rejection and abandonment. Needless to say, they feel insecure when interacting with another individual beyond the traditional social norm. Moreover, their romantic relationships are punctuated by a distant and avoidant nature. These are the folks who are generally emotionally unavailable. In such relationships, dismissive avoidant adult will strive to keep everyone at arm's length. The idea is that if you let someone get too close, they will end up hurting you one way or another.

Anxious preoccupied attachment

This is the type of attachment in which relationships and bonds are formed, yet they are rooted in security and anxiety. The anxiety mainly stems from abandonment issues. As such, the anxious preoccupied individual will do everything in their power to solve and fix the problems of the other party. This could be a spouse, partner, children, siblings, friends, virtually anyone. The point is to create a type of co-dependence in which they can ensure that they won't become easily abandoned by those close to them. This can lead to unhealthy relationships in which one party is totally reliant on the other. That being said, the other party may decide to take advantage of the anxious preoccupied individual and demand more and more every time. Some telltale signs are excessive jealousy, possessiveness and overall clingy and neediness.

Fearful avoidant attachment

In this type of relationship, the fearful avoidant individual will generally try to run away from their feelings and emotions. They are afraid of being hurt, being let down or simply being disappointed by the way their relationships may turn out. So, they rather tune out rather than become engaged and involved in the relationship itself. These folks are prone to moodiness and unpredictable behavior. They may often become diagnosed with a disorder such as bipolar disorder though such cases are rather extreme. Nevertheless, there is a good chance that these individuals will develop negatively charged relationships. Needless to say, the end result can lead to unhealthy attachments that will become detrimental to all parties involved.

As you can see, attachment styles can truly have a considerable impact on the way you conduct yourself with others in your day-to-day relationships. Of course, there are some extreme cases in which some individuals are so dysfunctional that they cannot connect with others even at a basic level.

Moreover, it is also common to manifest some traits of all of these attachment styles especially if you came from a dysfunctional family dynamic. Certainly, it is not your fault that your family life developed in one way or another, but it is up to you to make the best of your current situation. After all, you have nothing to lose and everything to gain.

Identifying attachment issues

Now that we have discussed the various attachment styles, the time has come to identify which of these attachment styles best applies to you. Consequently, we will be doing a small test (yes, a test!). This is simple and all it requires is for you to check the answer that best suits your own personal feelings. So, please take a moment to read them and then choose the one which best suits you.

I am not normally comfortable around others. It is hard for me to trust others at times. It is also hard for me to show that I can rely on them. I get very nervous when anyone comes too close to me. There are times when others want a more intimate relationship than I am able to handle.

It is rather easy for me to relate to others. I don't really have much trouble getting close to others or letting others get close to me. I am not concerned about being abandoned or otherwise neglected. I feel that I can relate to others on a very personal level.

I find it that others are hesitant to get close to me. I also find it very hard to let others get close to me. I am worried that my partner will leave and won't want to come back to me. I don't have very many friends because I tend to be clingy and reliant on social interaction all the time in order to feel better about myself.

I feel that is it better to keep others at bay. I don't care about feelings and emotions. In fact, I believe that it is better to avoid developing any kind of attachment to others. After all, they might leave and never come back. In romantic relationships, it is better not to fall in love because you will always risk having a broken heart.

Reread these statements if you must. Please select the one that you are surest of. Now, it might be that you feel you can relate to more than one of these statements. However, please take the time to really make up your mind on which one you feel best describes the way you think and feel about developing attachment to others. Once you have made up your mind, we can then proceed to discussing the meaning behind them.

This statement refers to fearful and avoidant individuals. As you can see, it is mainly related to trust issues. When you feel this way, it is very hard for you to develop a strong bond with anyone as fear always echoes in the back of your mind. This will lead you to push people away or maintain a constantly suspicious and insecure attitude about everyone with whom you related yourself.

This statement refers to secure individuals. The statement speaks for itself. Note that there is a strong component of trust and understanding which underscores the nature of such relationships. If you happen to become engaged in a relationship with this type of person, regardless of the nature of the relationship, you will find that they are genuinely concerned about you and they have everyone's best interest at heart. They are the consummate team player.

This statement refers to the anxious preoccupied individual. If you happen to engage in a relationship with this type of person, you will find that their clinginess stems from their ultimate fear of being neglected and abandoned. In men, this type of attachment style can be seen in overly possessive and jealous behavior of their partners. Additionally, you may find that they tend to micromanage just about everything in their lives. In the case of women, they tend to become overbearing and domineering. They are also the type of parents who become obsessed with every aspect of their children's lives.

This statement refers to the dismissive avoidant individual. These individuals tend to be the mysterious type. No one is ever good enough for them. They make it seem that it is because they have such high standards. This tends to be typical of very attractive or successful people. However, there might an underlying issue; it might be that you are dealing with an individual who is simply afraid of having their feelings hurt. This type of attachment tends to develop especially when the individual has gotten close to others in the past and has been hurt. Needless to say, their fear leads them to avoid any type of close relationships.

Whichever one of these types you happen to identify with, it is highly recommended that you take some time out to really ponder if you really feel this way. As you begin to uncover bits and pieces of information and experiences which you may have filed away for eternity, you will become more keenly aware of why you act and react the way you do.

It is very common to go for years without truly pinpointing many of these issues. You may find it hard to believe that you really do act a certain way. But when you do, it might be time to find a way to improve upon yourself. After all, a negative attachment style may lead you to push your twin flame away especially when they are trying to get close to you. It goes without saying that the last thing you want to do is drive them away.

Keeping a journal of your feelings and emotions

One of the most effective exercises which you can use to help you identify any potential attachment issues is keeping a diary.

Now, we are not talking about "Dear Diary" type of journaling. This type of journaling is more about keeping track of your feelings, particularly in specific moments and situations.

For example, you went on a date today. You met with someone whom you like and find attractive. As such, the purpose of the journal entry is to record your feelings throughout the event.

Keeping in mind the following questions:

How did I feel throughout the event?

Was I nervous, anxious, worried, or concerned about anything?

Did I feel detached like it wasn't important?

How did the other person react to my attitude?

Did they say or do anything that I didn't like?

Did I do anything they didn't like?

These are some general questions which can help you keep track of your reactions and behavior. As you begin to gain more practice and experience with journaling, you will see how your own self-assessment will enable you to make keen insights into your own actions and reactions.

This type of self-observation is just another way in which you can live in the here and now. By eliminating unneeded stress from your life, you can focus on becoming the type of person others like to be around.

If you feel that your interactions are generally good, then journaling will help you to keep track on what's working and what could be improved. Please bear in mind that nothing is perfect in life. So, keeping track of your day-to-day interactions will help you improve upon the good things that you are already doing.

Ultimately, your ability to spot any potential attachment issues and then begin to work on them will enable you to become the best version of yourself. After all, it certainly pays to take the time and work on yourself. By improving upon your current strengths and bolstering your weaknesses, you can open the door to wonderful and meaningful relationships. While these relationships may not become anything close to your twin flame, they will provide you with great opportunities to get to know great people.

How to know when you are ready to begin to let go

The flip side of attachment is letting go.

Since virtually all attachment issues stem from childhood or traumatic events, there will come a time when you need to let go in order to begin healing any issues which may be preventing your from developing strong and meaningful relationships.

As you progress in journey toward self-discovery, you will eventually come to a point where you will feel comfortable in confronting the issues that have impacted your life. Whatever such events may be, one of the most significant ways in which you can break through blockages for good is by facing that very situation that caused you to build up emotional blockages.

As we have discussed before, you will feel instinctively ready to confront people, places and even objects which have haunted you all this time. Nevertheless, it is not just in confronting the facts that will make your issues disappear. It is merely the beginning.

However, it should be celebrated as the momentous event that it is.

It is never easy to face your tormentors. It is never easy to face your fears head on.

Yet, there will come a time when you must begin to let go. The emotional burden that comes with holding on to the memories of painful events can become too much to bear. As such, resolving to let go can be one of the biggest decisions you will ever make in your life. And when you do, when you make that decision, you will feel like a ton of bricks has been removed off your shoulders.

Then, the healing process can begin.

It may take a while, or it might be faster than you think. Whatever the circumstances, you will be able to find yourself underneath the layers of needless baggage. The journey to self-discovery is all about cutting through the jungle of your mind and finding the hidden treasure. There is no doubt that there is no treasure more valuable than finding your essence, that inner being which may be locked up somewhere.

As you find your way through to your inner being, the various parts of yourself will begin to line up in perfect harmony. As you begin achieving wholeness, you will start feeling a sensation of peace. Sure, there are always obstacles along the way. But as you reconnect with all facets of your being, you will feel invincible.

While that may sound a bit dramatic, it is actually true. There is nothing more comforting in this world than knowing who you are, what you want and where you want to be. In the end, you hold the roadmap that will lead to your ultimate happiness and a reunion with your beloved twin flame.

Chapter 10: Letting go of attachment

"Love is but the discovery of ourselves in another, and the delight in the recognition."

-- Alexander Smith

As we have discussed earlier, attachment is about holding on to things and people. Often, these attachments don't lead us to anything positive. If anything, they perpetuate negative feelings as observed in the various attachment styles.

The journey through attachments is often bumpy and filled with obstacles. But when you have made up your mind to let go, you will not only letting go of many of the things and people holding you back, you will find peace and comfort.

Being able to let go is also a skill.

This skill will come into practice any time you have changes to deal with. For example, you might have to sell your old car and get a new one because the old one doesn't work anymore. Yet, you are so attached to your old car, that it makes no sense to get another one. Yet, your old car keeps breaking down and the cost of repairing it is greater than the cost of buying a new one.

Nevertheless, you are so attached to your old car that you will sink as much money as you can in order to keep it running. Naturally, such an attitude is counterproductive since it only serves to drain on your resources rather than helping you have reliable transportation.

So, part of understanding attachment is knowing that the time will come when you have to let go of everything and everyone around you.

The sunk cost fallacy

Have you ever heard of the sunk cost fallacy?

In essence, a sunk cost is an amount of resources which you spend on something which you will never get back.

Let's continue discussing cars.

If you purchase a car for $100, you can expect to lose value on the car over time. As such, you will not get $100 by the time you decide to sell. You will end up getting far less than what you paid for. However, things get complicated when the car begins to break down. As you start putting money into it, you realize that you have spent too much money on it.

Nevertheless, you are wary of selling it because of the fact that you have put too much money into it already. In addition, since you understand that you are not going to get much for it, you begin to obsess with keeping the car and making it look nice.

The fact of the matter is that you will never recoup the money you have put into care. All you will end up with is a very expensive problem. Since you are unable to dump the car, you end up sinking money into it with the hope of getting it to run properly again.

Eventually, you will end up realizing that if you had saved the money that you spent in fixing the old car, you would have been able to buy a new car. So, on top of losing the money you spent in fixing the old car, now you have to spend money on buying a new one.

This concept of the sunk cost fallacy is also applicable to relationships.

In this case, it is common for people to remain in a relationship for a longer period of time since they feel that the investment in time and effort they have already put into a relationship is not worth throwing away. Therefore, they keep putting time and effort into the relationship in hopes of saving it or improving it when it is clear that it is not going anywhere. This type of attitude can only lead to further disappointment and frustration.

As you can see, the sunk cost fallacy leads individuals to continue to spend time and effort into a relationship, be it romantic, friendship or a business relationship, that is not producing any gains but rather is only a source of frustration and anxiety.

Thus, the most important thing to keep in mind when you find yourself in a toxic, or otherwise unproductive relationship, is to cut your losses. This can be a very difficult decision to make as cutting your losses can be the source of a profound disappointment. It can lead you to think that you have wasted a great deal of your time on preserving a relationship that did not pay off as you would expect. However, there comes a time when you must cut your losses and move on.

Think about a regular business. If you are running a business and it is not paying the profits that you expect, you have to make a choice. Either you continue in the business and try your best or you shut things down and move on to something which you feel can provide you with the results that you would like.

This is a very tough choice.

For some people, it is really hard to let go. After all, imagine investing effort, time, dedication, and even love into a situation which may not be providing you with the outcomes you feel you deserve. Yet, there are times when you simply need to move on.

At the end of the day, it is mainly a question of making the conscious choice to let go. When you make up your mind to let go, you are opening the door for true healing to take place especially if you are clinging to a negative experience which has marked your life in a deep and profound way.

As such, let's take a look at five practical tips which you can use to help you let go of an attachment and improve upon your own personal attachment style.

Tip #1: Just admit it

This is, by far, the hardest thing to do.

For instance, if you are a clingy person, it can be hard to admit that you are clingy. After all, no one likes to admit they hang on too much. Most people will try to pretend that it is not true even if they are told multiple times by multiple people that they are clingy and won't let go easily.

This is quite evident in romantic relationships. When two people meet, one, or even both, may turn out to be clingy and needy. What this leads to is suffocating the other partner. The clingy individual will consistently seek more and more attention while the other party will become overwhelmed by the increasing demand for attention and acknowledgment.

If you have ever gone through the painful experience of a breakup because you were too clingy, jealous or possessive, then you can understand how difficult a separation can be. It opens up all kinds of wounds. It can lead you to feeling desperate. Such feelings can lead the needy individual to attempt anything in order to keep their partner from leaving them. Needless to say, this only feeds the clingy attitude that led to the breakup in the first place.

When you admit to yourself that your attitude is too possessive, then you are able to start looking into the reasons why you act in this way. While it is hardly an easy road, just the fact that you are starting out on the road to wholeness is a lot better than doing nothing.

On the flip side, if you happen to be surrounded by one, or more, clingy individuals, then you might want to look at pulling yourself out of that situation. You might find that the toll such relationships are taking on you may end up feeding attachment feelings of your own. It is rather easy to fall into a trap like this yourself. So, it is definitely worth pulling yourself away from such circumstances.

As we have stated earlier, living in the present and the now will help you identify the times when these feelings emerge. When they do, you can then make a note of it. If you get jealous, possessive and/or clingy feelings several times a day, then make a note of it.

When you begin to identify the triggers, you can begin to visualize why you do it. This will lead to understanding why you feel the way you do. Ultimately, you will be able to hit a breakthrough. This breakthrough may very well reveal the reasons for the way you feel.

Tip #2: Understanding your feelings

When tip #1 begins to bear fruit, you will start to gain insights into your feelings of attachment. Of course, you will encounter many uncomfortable feelings at first. After all, you are making yourself vulnerable. Even if your vulnerabilities are not public, they are still floating to the surface. This can be a scary and very intimidating experience. You may find yourself reliving some unpleasant and even traumatic experiences. This is why you need to have some kind of support system around you.

With the help of close friends and family, or the help of a trusted professional, you can begin to open up. As you open up, you will begin to recognize what brings about these feelings. This is where journaling plays a key role in understanding your feelings.

It's one thing to recognize your feelings and the triggers. But it is a completely different thing when you are able to pinpoint the exact causes of your feelings. Since you are fully immersed in this situation, it might be hard to commit the details of specific events to memory.

So, journaling can help you develop a record of your feelings. These can include triggers and the consequences of these events. Then, you can go back and look at the events and how they played out. Your journal can serve as a chronicle of the progress you have made over the course of a given time period.

The biggest resistance you might encounter from yourself is the belief that you are somehow better off being this way. For example, dismissive and avoidant individuals will find that having an aloof and vague nature will keep them from being hurt. By running away from their feelings, these individuals feel that they are protecting themselves from being hurt like they were in the past.

Naturally, it is never healthy to run away from feelings as they will invariably catch up with you at some point. Eventually, when your feelings do catch up with you, dealing with them can become a daunting task. This is why taking baby steps is often the easiest way of easing into one's feelings.

In cases where fear takes over, significant levels of stress and anxiety may build up to a point where you may not be able to cope. This is where a good support network can help you get through tough moments. For example, if you revisit a particular incident by going back to the scene where it happened, the last thing you want to do is go there on your own. Often, reliving memories can prove to be one of the hardest experiences you can put yourself through. As such, having loved ones who can support you will make facing your demons that much easier.

Ultimately, you may not be able to rid yourself of attachment feelings all together. But, you will eventually reach a place where you will be at peace with yourself and the circumstances in which you try to live through. This will allow you to come to grips with who you are. In a way, it is like a person who understands they must live with a condition. So, instead of getting down on themselves, they adapt to it and learn to live with their condition. In the end, they are able to live as best a life as they can give the existence of their condition.

Tips #3: Letting go of expectations and desires

One of the biggest killers in life are unmet expectations and unfulfilled desires.

Earlier, we discussed how expectations can put a serious damper on any relationship. They can break any deal especially when you have such high hopes. Then, in the blink of an eye, they can be dashed by human error. It sounds quite simple, but it truly is.

When you let expectations dictate the way you are going to go about your relationships, then you are opening the door for disappointments. Now, this isn't to say that you shouldn't have any expectations at all. What it does mean is that you need to manage your expectations so that they are realistic.

Nevertheless, there are unmet expectations that we just can't let go of. In fact, there are folks that feel like the world owes them something. For instance, these are folks that believe that because they didn't have something growing up, or never got the chance to do something, they go around blaming everyone and everything for the things which haven't gone their way. They feel entitled to getting certain things and being certain things in life.

If you feel that you deserve this, that and the other, just because you didn't have it when you were younger, then you might be up for disappointment. If you feel that you deserve to find your twin flame, you are right, but for the wrong reason.

You see, you don't *have to* find your twin flame. There's nothing that says that this is a must. What you must aspire is to find your twin flame because you *want to*. This is what makes the reunion so magical and special. But if you feel that this is something that you have coming to you, then you might not feel compelled to work on improving yourself for the sake of your relationship.

A similar situation may happen to you if you are carrying unfulfilled desires around.

Naturally, there are things that we all want. There are situations that we want to go our way. However, we can't always get what we want. Yet, it can be really hard to accept the things that we can't get or haven't gone our way.

Yet, having unfilled desires clouding our judgement can lead us to make the wrong choices. For example, if an individual feels that they haven't gotten the attention that they want, they will lash out in ways that they feel will get the attention they seek.

This is when you see some folks abusing drugs or doing reckless actions. They do it, not because they like it, or they feel they will gain something out of it. They do it to get attention. And when they do get it, that only feeds this behavior further.

If there is something in your life which you still haven't gotten, make up your mind to get it through whatever means you have at your disposal. But if you sit back sulking about why it hasn't happened to you, then you will only contribute to the divide between you and your higher self. The most important thing which you can do is give your higher being a chance to communicate with by clearing the road of any needless resentment.

Tip #4: Care for yourself

The previous tips are centered around what might seem like a selfish attitude. However, there are cases in which you might have the opposite attitude. You are so concerned about others that you don't really care for yourself.

Now, this isn't a case such as people pleasers who are trying to do anything they can to get others to like them. This is the type of situation in which an individual may be so concerned with others, such as their family, that they don't really pay attention to their own needs. This leads to a disconnect between the body and mind with your higher being. This disconnect stems from the fact that you are more concerned about the wellbeing of others as compared to your own.

Think about this situation:

You work really hard to put food on the table and provide for your family. You are in constant control of everything that happens at work and home. You always try your best to make sure that your loved ones get what they need. Yet, who is concerned about what you need? Who puts your needs ahead of theirs?

In the short run, it is not that bad. It is perfectly fine to shift your focus to those who need attention more than you do. However, this attitude becomes a problem when you don't get the attention and care you need. This may become evident with your health. You may end up suffering from health issues simply because you neglected to take better care of yourself.

After a while, this becomes a cycle. You may even end up feeling guilty about putting yourself first at times. But please bear in mind that if something should happen to you, your loved ones would miss you. Not only that, but they would be left without an important part of their lives. And while money and material possessions are essential to ensuring survival, they are not the only things in life.

After all, how many people have you heard regret not having spent more time at the office while on their deathbed? No one regrets missing days at work. Yet, everyone regrets the time they lost while being away from their loved ones.

Consequently, this tip is meant to encourage you to put yourself first sometimes. Get the rest you need and get the nutrition your body demands. You will not be much use to your twin flame if you are constantly tired and moody. In addition, if you become sick, for whatever reason, take the time to recover. There are plenty of things in life which can wait. But your health and overall wellbeing should not be one of them.

So, don't neglect yourself. Of course, it is commendable that you put others ahead of you, the ones who truly need you, need you in tip-top shape. Thus, take the time to mind your health and your wellbeing. Your loved ones, especially your twin flame, will be much better off for it.

Tip #5: Embrace positive thinking

Your future will be molded by the thoughts you think and the words you say. We have already talked about the power of affirmations and visualization.

Nevertheless, there is no amount of affirmations and visualization that can overcome what you actually think and feel.

For instance, let's say that you want to pass an exam at school. This exam will open the door for you to graduate. It is one of the hardest tests you will face since this class isn't your strong suit. So, you prepare with the power of affirmations. You visualize being successful in the exam. Yet, when the time comes for you to actually do the test, you find yourself excessively nervous.

Why?

Because you don't feel confident you can make it. Somewhere deep inside of you, you don't think you have what it takes to make it.

So, you have a contradiction here. On the one hand, you declare and visualize that you can do it. But inside, you are unsure and insecure about the outcome of the test. Of course, your vision and declarations are very powerful. But if you don't truly believe it inside of you, you won't be as successful as you'd hope to be.

What can you do to improve this?

For starters, you can begin to practice positive thinking. Embrace positive thinking.

You can start by removing all of the negative words in your vocabulary. Stop using expressions such as "can't," "couldn't," "won't" or "unable." These are all negative expressions which will fuel negative experiences.

But if you accompany your affirmations and visualization with positive thinking, then everything will begin to fall into place. You will see how your declarations are like seeds falling in fertile ground. You will also see how your visions will eventually come true.

This is why you cannot afford to neglect any aspect of your psyche. The more in tune you are with your feelings and your higher self, you will be able to translate your positive thinking in actions.

Moreover, the best way to combat the enemy of positive thinking, that is, pessimistic thoughts, is to face your negative thoughts head on. If you fail the exam, what else could you do to pass the class? Can you take a make-up exam? Is there a chance that you can gain some extra credit by writing a paper?

If you do the math, you will see that over 90% of our worries are unfounded. You will see that the fears you have aren't as bad as they might seem. The most important thing to keep in mind is that you need to be ready for anything that might come your way.

Positive thinking is the cornerstone of all successful people. Truly successful individuals believe that they will become successful.

The same case applies to your twin flame; if you keep a positive attitude and mindset, this will serve a beacon for them to find you. So, you can start making the road easier for your twin flame today by lighting up the way with your positive thoughts.

Part III: Recognizing and living your twin flame

Chapter 11: Recognizing a true twin flame encounter

"The most wonderful of all things in life, I believe, is the discovery of another human being with whom one's relationship has a glowing depth, beauty, and joy as the years increase. This inner progressiveness of love between two human beings is a most marvelous thing, it cannot be found by looking for it or by passionately wishing for it. It is a sort of divine accident."

-- Hugh Walpole

This entire book has been leading up to this moment. This is the moment in which one half of a twin flame meets its other half. And while this moment may not be filled with fireworks as some might seem to believe, it is a beautiful and magical moment, nonetheless.

So, when you discover your twin flame, you will discover them as a wonderful human being that you had no idea existed, but that you knew was always there. In fact, it might be the culmination of a long, personal journey which led you to this point.

Now, you are ready to walk, hand in hand, with the new human being. Regardless of the nature of this relationship, the magic and the chemistry are undeniable. You are the epitome of what it means to become one.

That is why this chapter is devoted to understanding what a twin flame encounter is and how you can recognize some of the signs. In doing so, you will be able to determine if you have actually been part of such an encounter.

When twin flames meet, and recognition happens at a deep and spiritual level, the energies of both beings begin to purge, or cut out, energies that don't mesh with each other's frequencies. This is also known as the "soul song." A soul song is nothing more than the inner frequency of an individual's core being.

As such, both parts of the twin flame become in synch. Therefore, there is no doubt that these two halves mesh with each other on a deep and meaningful level. You can perceive this in the way both halves automatically seem to come into perfect harmony with one another, except that it may not be perceptible at a superficial level.

In addition, the main purpose of the twin flame reunion is to elevate both parts' vibrations in order to eliminate past negativity, pain, suffering and any other type of negative energy. When this occurs, the moment of ascension begins to take place.

Under these circumstances, both halves may find themselves having to deal with all the baggage that comes with digging up the past. Needless to say, digging up the past is not a pleasant situation. However, a false flame will make a case of the past whereas a twin flame will help their other half overcome any issues that may have been brought back to the forefront.

It is at this point, when dealing with the past and old baggage, that the relationship may become too much for one, or both parties, and then the running and chasing dynamic begins. In this dynamic, one twin flame runs away from the scene while the other is left to chase after them.

This dynamic is not ideal, and it happens when one of the flames is not exactly ready to take on the role of becoming a dedicated and committed twin flame. The reasons for this are numerous. So, it then becomes essential for the runner to think about why they are running away. If they are running away from themselves, it might be a sign of a greater issue that still needs to be resolved.

We will discuss the runner and chaser dynamic in a later chapter. For now, it is worth mentioning that the ascension process, the result of the twin flame encounter and reunion, will bring about old insecurities and issues. This is why a true twin flame will be an ally in the process.

It is also worth noting that when the runner and chaser dynamic begins to take place, it can become easy to dismiss as true twin flame for a false twin flame. After all, false flames tend to bail out when things get rough. But don't fret, real twin flame always end up making their way back to each other.

On the whole, twin flame encounters are one of the most exciting and wonderful moments in any person's life. This is why it is important to have a good idea of what to expect if and when it happens. If you don't have a good idea about what can happen, you may miss the encounter. This could lead you to drop the ball and miss recognizing your twin flame. In fact, the worst thing that could happen is that you end up dismissing your twin flame simply because you didn't pick up on the signs.

So, we are going to be taking a look at nine telltale signs about a twin flame encounter. These signs are not so much about recognizing if a person is your twin flame or not, this is more about recognizing the actual encounter itself. This is where you can figure out if the dynamic and interaction between the two of you is indicative of a true twin flame encounter.

As such, we are going to dig a little bit deeper, so you know what to look for in that initial twin flame encounter.

Sign #1: Your heart is telling you this is it

When your heart begins to race, it is usually because you are excited in some type of manner. Now, in a twin flame encounter, your heart will automatically tip you off. Bear in mind that this isn't about meeting someone good-looking or attractive. This is about meeting the real thing.

In general, when you meet someone who is good-looking, your heart tends to be a bit faster as a product of the attraction. In this case, however, it is not the usual rise in blood pressure that accompanies meeting someone attractive. This is a "glowing" feeling that is telling you that you are in the presence of the one.

Furthermore, you will find you get all of the signs at an instinctive level. Your heart is sending you a message that you have connected. This is why twin flame encounters are usually described as unique. Most folks described them as experiences in which they met someone they could not help but admire and find usually interesting.

Please bear in mind that when talking about romantic twin flame encounters, the reaction will be consistent with meeting a potential mate. However, when the relationship is not romantic, the signs will still be there. You will feel as though you met someone whom you cannot stop thinking about.

So, don't shut your heart out. It will give you the best clue as to how to identify your twin flame.

Sign #2: Immediate eye contact

One of the most common ways in which folks can identify a twin flame encounter is by making eye contact.

Now, we always make eye contact with various people. Sometimes, you make eye contact with someone you dislike. Therefore, the contact is brief and may even lead to sending the wrong message.

In the case of a twin flame encounter, we are talking about a deep gaze that tells you everything you need to know about the other person.

In a romantic context, this gaze may lead to an immediate sense of attraction and chemistry. And while the meeting may happen outside a social context (for example in a business meeting, seminar, or other professional situation), the chemistry is unavoidable.

In non-romantic relationships, this gaze can be more of an acknowledgement. A way of recognizing that you know who they are. This is very common in friends of the same gender. Since there would be no romantic feelings between them, the stare can be more of a way of signaling that they are on the same page.

This gaze is often described as "looking into the other person's soul." But here's the kicker: since you are two parts of the same soul, it's like looking into a "mirror soul." You can look into virtually anyone's soul. But this encounter is like looking at your own reflection.

Sign #3: A different dimension

When the twin flame encounter occurs, one of the most common ways of describing it is "entering a different dimension." Usually, this sensation is like having the outside world disappear and just leaving both flames standing there, next to each other.

In cases where you have already met your twin flame, but just not realized it was them, the moment of realization is that first moment when you are transported to that other dimension. This is where you take off and join each other at a much deeper level. Consequently, the whole world seems to fade away around you.

One other interesting way in which this encounter is described is by having time stop. When time stops, it's like there is nothing else happening at the moment. It's just the two flames finally getting reacquainted.

The psychological perception of time stopping is due to the spiritual connection that takes place when both flames are together. This stoppage of time is not just at the moment of meeting. It is common to experience it whenever the two flames come together. As such, stopping time is more a product of the deep level of fascination between both parts rather than just an old-fashioned attraction.

Other ways of describing this different dimension is through getting a sensation of becoming more aware of the inner self, but also of everything around the two flames. This represents a heightened sense of awareness. Thus, everything seems to come into better focus. Everything seems to become clearer and easier to understand.

This is where the ascension process begins to take shape. This is where both halves become attuned to their higher selves thereby producing that instant connection.

Sign #4: Empathy

This can only be described as an uncanny sense of understanding and synchronization. This is where both parts make the most of their connection and begin to connect and accept each other unconditionally.

This is key.

There are no conditions. There are no limitations in the relationship among twin flames. There is only love and appreciation for each other. Of course, there might be differences. In fact, there might be huge differences. But that won't stop them from finding the right groove between each other. They will immediately hit it off.

Therefore, the level of empathy between twin flames is undeniable. If one is not doing well, the other will certainly pick up on it. In these types of relationships, one can immediately tell what's going on with the other. They won't have to guess what's wrong. They will immediately pick up on something out of the ordinary.

By the same token, one will be receptive to the other's happiness and joy. This perception will only lead to them feeding off each other in such a way that they will be able to connect and share their feelings. This creates a positive feedback loop that enriches the soul.

That is why this concept of empathy is about both the good and the bad times.

Sign #5: An intuitive feel

When you meet your twin flame, there is an intuitive feel about your meeting. The difference between the heart speaking to you and an intuitive feel is that your heart will signal that this is the one. Your heart will come yell, "this is it!"

On the flip side, the intuitive feel of this person makes it seem like you don't need to get to know them; you already know them. As such, you may not have to ask them what they like to drink. You already have a feeling they like the same drinks as you. Or, you won't have to guess what music they like, what food they enjoy or even what things they dislike. All of this seems like it has been preprogrammed.

It is because of this intuitive feel that the relationship between twin flames progresses very quickly. If this is a regular friendship, they become very close, very quickly. They won't be guessing about who they are or what they stand for. They are already keenly aware of all these factors.

In fact, a false flame encounter may leave you feeling amazed and admiring this person you have just met. But you won't automatically pick up on them. You might even find some of their reactions and behaviors to be strange or quirky. This is your intuition telling you that they are not the one.

Sign #6: Chakra activation

This sign is so subtle that it might be virtually imperceptible.

When your chakras become activated, they produce various reactions in your being. For instance, you might feel privy to information no one is. You feel like you understand everything that's going on. You are completely in the loop.

Since your heart is screaming at you, your heart chakra may very well be going into overdrive. As such, your heart chakra may produce a tingling sensation in your chest. Additionally, you may find that your entire body is producing a warm feeling that runs across your limbs, or your face.

Another important effect of chakra activation is the heightened sense of awareness you get. You will become more in synch with everything around you especially your twin flame. That is why we discussed chakras earlier in this book.

If you should have chakra blockages, then you might not get the full benefit of your twin flame encounter. You might even miss this sign and not recognize your twin flame. Thus, clearing your chakras of ill energy is vital in order to take advantage of every moment you spend with your twin flame.

Sign #7: Inexplicable connection

When you meet your twin flame, an inexplicable connection automatically goes online. This connection is often described as a flash, sort of like a lightning strike. Other times, it is described as electricity running through one's body.

Indeed, this inexplicable connection cannot be easily described in words. It is just something that is there. It is a link that just happens without having to think about it. This is the consequence of meeting your twin flame.

That is why earlier sections of this book have been dedicated toward helping you find that balance in both your mind and body. That is why emotional blockages are so detrimental to twin flame relationships. Such blockages will wreak havoc on the connection between twin flames rendering it inoperable.

As you begin to clear your emotions and chakras, this connection will happen smoothly and without hesitation. At the end of the day, the end result will be a connection that cannot be expressed in simple terms.

Sign #8: Magnetic

Another word used to describe this encounter is "magnetic."

Now, it is one thing to feel attracted to someone. However, a magnetic pull will not allow you to separate from this person. Thus, you are completely drawn to them. Even if you wanted to pull away, it would be very hard to do so. You will not only feel drawn to your twin flame, but you will feel like you never left them.

Once the connection is setup, it will very hard to switch it off.

That is why the sense of magnetism between both flames, regardless of the nature of the relationship, is unavoidable. However, when there is a runner and chaser dynamic, what the runner attempts to do is avoid that magnetic pull. Yet, the pull is so strong that it ends up bringing them back together again.

Indeed, the connection between flames is about as strong as anything in life. It is undeniable and virtually impossible to destroy.

Sign #9: Wholeness

Perhaps the most important word used to describe this encounter is "wholeness."

The presence of your twin flame will give you a feeling of being whole; of being one. You are not separated. You are essentially acting as one. This is the real deal.

This sensation of wholeness is also described as joy, fulfillment and even bliss.

In romantic relationships, it is one lover consumed by the other and vice versa. In the case of non-romantic relationships, it is often described as a feeling of peace and calm. The mere presence of the twin flame is enough to leave the other feeling comforted and reassured.

The feeling of wholeness is essential during the ascension period. You see, given the baggage that might come up during this process, both flames need to rely on the other for support and companionship. This is where empathy and connectivity plan such a pivotal role throughout the process.

In the end, each flame can become reliant on the other for just about every type of need they may have. The spiritual and emotional parts are seemingly intertwined. As for the physical, there are limitations that the physical body may not be able to overcome, such as distance. Nevertheless, when two twin flames come together physically, both flames can feed off each other in ways that no one else can.

How to react during a possible twin flame encounter

The most important thing if you suspect you are having a twin flame encounter is to keep calm. You might get excited and feeling pumped up. However, an overly emotional reaction may lead you to put your twin flame on the edge.

In these cases, it is best to let things follow their course. If you don't push things, rather than just go with the flow, you will begin to see how your heart will lead you in. Then, you can allow all of these wonderful sensations to take place.

The end result will be a magical moment that you will cherish for the rest of your life.

Chapter 12: Identifying a false flame encounter

"When connections are real, they simply never die. They can be buried or ignored or walked away from, but never broken. If you've deeply resonated with another person or place, the connection remains despite any distance, time, situation, lack of presence, or circumstance. If you're doubtful then just try it – go and revisit a person or place and see if there's any sense at all of the space between now and then. If it was truly real, you'll be instantly swept back into the moment it was before it left – during the same year and place with the same wonder and hope, comfort and heartbeat. Real connections live on forever."

-- Victoria Erickson

Your twin flame relationship is really what most people refer to as their "soulmate" relationship. However, you can have many soulmates in the course of your lifetime, but only one twin flame. Your twin flame is your soul mirror. They share your "core soul frequency." That means that though your relationship is indeed blissful, it can also be difficult. No relationship brings you into a clearer awareness of yourself than this one.

That's why there's also false twin flame relationships. This is what happens when we find someone who we think is our perfect match, but really exists to help us identify and then clear karma and patterning so that we can be ready for the real thing. Here is how to tell the difference between the two.

That is why we are going to devote this chapter to discussing 16 signs that indicate you are experiencing a false flame and not your true, twin flame.

Sign #1: Both your true twin flame and your false twin flame are similar in many ways

In fact, when you are with your real twin flame, you will look back and realize that you identified a lot of their traits and characteristics in your former partner. You were perhaps temporarily confusing one person for another.

This is the one sign that leads to a great deal of confusion. On the one hand, you and your false flame are very similar. You have many of the same tastes and opinions, yet there are certain aspects that don't quite mesh together.

To further compound the confusion, your false flame and your true twin flame are very similar in a number of ways. So, it is very hard telling them apart. In general, the best way to tell them apart is by listening to your heart. When you do, you will be able to see who truly strikes a chord with you. Ultimately, you and your false flame may get along phenomenally well though there might be a deal breaker, or two, keeping you apart.

With your true twin flame, there are no deal breakers.

Sign #2: Your false flame digs up the past

When you're dealing with a soulmate, you will find that the issues arising largely have to do with past mistakes, anxieties, fears or concerns. With your twin flame, your issues will be more about what's going to happen, and how to fulfill your complete purpose while alive.

This is a very interesting point to consider. You might be confusing a soulmate relationship with a twin flame relationship. As such, your soulmate might be digging up bits of the past which are only meant to hurt you. If your twin flame brings up the past it is because they are there to help you grow and move on from it. Otherwise, there would be no point in digging up the past.

Please bear in mind that a false flame may help you overcome some issues from the past, but they will not be there to accompany you on your personal journey. In a way, they might provide you with a bit of a nudge rather than push you to become better and better.

Given the fact that false flames are intended to help you "awaken" and realize your potential, they may remind you of past experiences in order for you to address them. That way, you will be ready for when the time comes to meet your true twin flame. So, please be careful when a false flame leads you down such a road. It may lead to a very unpleasant encounter with things you might not be ready to deal with.

Sign #3: Your false flame will help you help yourself; your true twin flame will help you help others

False twins come into our lives when we need to become self-aware and create change for ourselves. True twins come when it's time for us to extend our powers out and start creating change in the lives of those around us.

Since a false flame has a very specific purpose in your life, it will be rather common to have them help you on the road to self-discovery. Now, you might think that they have an altruistic goal in mind. However, a false flame may provide you with a disastrous relationship. This disaster will lead you to reassess your perspective on life. In fact, it may lead you to question yourself and the way you have been doing things. Consequently, it leads you on the road to self-discovery.

In the case of a true twin flame, they will not only aid you in your journey of self-discovery, but they will also aid you in helping others. They may encourage you to take part in social causes or just simply become a better human being.

As such, your true twin flame will always find a way to push you to become a better person no matter what.

Sign #4: When the going gets tough, your false flame will fade away; your true twin flame will rise to the occasion

Something that ultimately separates the false flames from the true ones is that the false ones, well, fade. When you challenge each other and have disagreements, their true commitment will be revealed. Ultimately, they (or you) will walk away because it is "too hard." A true flame will be willing to endure anything to be with you.

This is a telltale sign that your twin flame is false, and your true twin flame is true. A true twin flame will always stand by you especially when things get tough. Think of the hardest moments in life. This is when your true twin flame will rise to the occasion and deliver what you expect from them. Imagine those situations in which your spouse, or perhaps your best friend, will come in and support you in a way you never thought possible.

Other times, you might be so out of it, that they can just take over and let you deal with whatever is going on. Please bear in mind that the main function of a twin flame is to walk with you and be by your side.

Sign #5: A false flame will cause anxiety and stress while your true twin flame will provide you with peace and calm

There will be a certain degree of comfort with your true twin that isn't present with a false one. They will feel like your best friend, as though you are finally coming back home after all this time.

Earlier, we mentioned how a true twin flame is meant to feel like home. They provide you with peace and harmony. They are not trying to cause any type of anxiety in you at all. Sure, there is always a degree of uncertainty especially if circumstances are not in your favor. But as long as you are with your twin flame, you will feel like you have never left home. They will be there to love you and give you the stability you need regardless of the type of relationship you may have.

Sign #6: Your relationship with a false flame will always hang in the balance whereas your relationship with your true twin flame will always be clearly defined even when difficult

The twin flame relationship is almost always characterized by a sort of back-and-forth, breaking up and then reuniting later. However, with a false twin, those breaks will be longer and more severe, and when you reunite, it will only be for a short period of time and won't end well.

A true twin flame will always tell you what they want and how they want it. Nevertheless, circumstances may not be the most conducive to your union. In the case of lovers, they might be met with incredible resistance. In this regard, they may have to fight against the odds. However, this doesn't mean that the relationship is not clearly defined. There will always be certainty as to where the relationship is headed.

Sign #7: A false flame relationship will always be surrounded by doubt and second guessing while a true twin flame will always provide you with a high degree of security

One of the biggest signs of a false twin flame is an ongoing and intense uncertainty. Though so many aspects of your relationship will seem like everything you've always looked for, there will be something in your mind and heart that questions whether or not this is really it. That won't happen with your true twin – at least, not as much.

This sign is more about yourself than your twin flame. A true twin flame will never lead you to question or second guess yourself. They will help you find the right answers when you need them. They won't cause you to feel unsure or perhaps insecure. A false flame will leave room for doubt since the foundation of your relationship may be shaky.

Sign #8: The purpose of a false flame is to "awaken" you; the purpose of a true twin flame is to help you ascend

Though the two terms can be used interchangeably at times, being awakened is beginning to recognize your inner power, and ascending is beginning to actually use it to create.

Awakening is part of the process of self-discovery. A false flame may provide you with the jolt that you need. However, a true twin flame will not only give you that jolt, they will walk with you as you begin to discover what is going on. In fact, they won't back down if you are having serious emotional distress as a result of counseling or therapy. They will be supportive and loving. The last thing they will do is judge you.

Consequently, ascension then becomes you making the next level on your journey through life. In fact, your true twin flame might be waiting for you on the other side of the bridge you need to cross.

Sign #9: A false flame will always make you doubt about whether you are meant to be together at some point; your true twin flame will always make their intentions known and clear

A false twin will always seem to be just a little out of reach, and you'll have to hold on just a little too tight to keep things going. With a true twin, the relationship is natural and effortless.

If you happen to find yourself doubting about whether they are the one and if this is the real thing, then chances are it is not. When it is the real thing, it just is. There are no questions and there is no second guessing. All it is, is your relationship taking off and progressing smoothly. You won't have to go out on a limb for your true twin flame. Things will fall into place without missing a beat.

Sign #10: A false flame means false hope while a true twin flame relationship will be unlike anything you have ever lived before

You'll be heartbroken to discover that your false twin seems to have these magical connections with, well, people who aren't you. It will be clear that your true twin has never had a relationship even close to what you have together, and they'll be cognizant of that fact, too.

This is why false flames always provide this sense of elusiveness. This elusiveness makes it feel like your relationship is "so close yet so far away." This makes it seem like you have nowhere to go. There isn't a natural progression in your relationship regardless of the nature of it. So, you don't get that sense that this is it, but rather, you get a sense of doubt and uncertainty about where you two will ultimately end up.

Sign #11: A false flame may feel threatened by your success; a true twin flame will draw energy from it and push you to excel

False twin flames are, of course, very similar to you, and you will probably be drawn to each other because you are so much alike. However, when you start to see success, a false twin will make you feel guilty for it, or think they are "losing" something. A true twin won't only be completely thrilled for you, they'll be playing an integral part of what's helping you succeed.

If you find that your partner, or best friend, ends up competing with you, then you are in the presence of a false flame. Your true twin flame may even do the exact same job as you. But rather than compete with you, they will find a way to help you rise above your limitations and become everything you could be. So, your twin flame is looking to make you feel so good about yourself and your skills, that they won't leave doubt about your abilities and talents.

Sign #12: A false flame is about helping you survive while your true twin flame is about helping you thrive

A false twin flame will be the very beginning of your awakening process. They'll reveal to you old wounds, patterns and habits that are really holding you back. Your true twin flame will not so much show you your leftover pain as they will help you see what it would take to live a completely aligned and abundant life.

Thus, your true twin flame will help you continuously become the best you can be. The main characteristic of a true twin flame relationship is that they will be supportive whatever you are doing. For instance, if you are looking to lose some weight, they will become an exercise buddy. They will go on a diet with you. And, they may even hold you accountable for the times you break your diet. But make no mistake, they have your best interest at heart.

Sign #13: A false flame will motivate you to go on your journey along while a true twin flame will go on the journey with you

One crucial difference between the two is that the false twin relationship tends to only awaken one of the partners. The true twin relationship awakens both, at the same time.

A false flame relationship is all about you, that is, helping you figure out about yourself. This circumstance is all about helping you figure out as much as you can about yourself. They will nudge you in the right direction. Beyond that, it's up to you.

Regarding your true twin flame, they won't just tell you or help you with a friendly nudge. They will walk with you and work with you to achieve your goals. Since you have the same goals in mind, they will walk along you, side by side. This is not about just joining you on the path; this is about going through the same experience as you. Look at it this way: they are not just cheering for you on the sidelines, they are there with you, on the field.

Sign #14: You don't always see eye to eye with a false flame on your lives' vision

Your false twin will always seem to be slightly on a different page than you. You don't have the same long-term vision, or at least, you can't seem to happily compromise for the other.

This one is a biggie. When you don't see eye to eye about your vision for the future and your life's goals, then you know that you are in the presence of a false flame. Your false flame may support you though they won't buy in. Your true twin flame will always be on the same page as you. What this means is that even if they don't like something, they will find a way to compromise. The point is to always be together no matter what.

Sign #15: A false flame relationship may leave you wondering if this is really happening to you; a true twin flame will make the purpose of the relationship clear to you

With your false twin flame, you'll wonder why you're experiencing so much pain and discord. With your true twin flame, you'll understand that sometimes, discomfort is crucial to growth, but that ultimately, you are working on yourself in order to be better for your relationship, the people around you, and of course, yourself.

This point is clear. Your true twin flame will always make it clear where they stand. There is no wondering or attempting to make heads or tails of the situation. With your true twin flame, you will always know where you stand.

Sign #16: A false flame will always have an excuse for not committing

Your true twin relationship will happen in spite of anything that could stand in the way. There is no barrier, no time constraint, no plan or preference that would make a true flame not be in a relationship with you... and that, in the end, is how you really know the difference.

While a false flame relationship may change you in a profound and meaningful way, it will be marked by a beginning and an end. With your true twin flame, there is no beginning. So, there is no end. You might leave each other. But you will invariably reunite at some point. And when you do, you will pick up right where you left of. In a way, twin flame relationships are like chapters in a book. One chapter may end, but the story continues.

Chapter 13: 18 signs you have met your twin flame

"When you're in love, you're capable of learning and knowing things you had never dared to think because love is the key to understanding of all mysteries."

-- Paulo Coelho

We have gone on an incredible journey throughout this book. We have discussed a journey of self-discovery and exploration. We have touched on some subjects that are a bit unpleasant. But we have also talked about some of the more sublime aspects of human existence.

In part III of this book, we are going to focus on what happens when you reunite with your twin flame. The key to this reunion is recognizing them. If you are able to recognize your twin flame, then you will be able to get started on the most exciting journey you can imagine.

Of course, not all twin flame relationships are the same. They are, however, built around the same premise: love and understanding.

Whether your twin flame is a lover, a friend, a relative or someone you meet by a twist of fate, you will be able to build an ever-lasting relationship predicated on supporting each other on the next leg of your journey. Naturally, you are together not just to support and collaborate, but also to push each other to excel at everything you do.

When you enter this type of partnership with your twin flame, you will be turbocharging yourself into truly becoming the best version you can be.

In this chapter, we are going to discuss 18 signs that will lead you to recognize your twin flame.

Sign #1: There is an intense attraction

This had to be the first sign.

Without any real cause or reason, you feel as though you've known this person before, even if you just met. The attraction is mutual and there is no reason to believe that you cannot, somehow, be united at a much deeper level. If you are in a romantic, twin flame relationship, everyone around you will notice your spark right away. They may even back off since the attraction is so intense there is no way anyone is going to get a word in edgewise.

If you are in a friendly relationship, you will become the ultimate pair, a "dynamic duo" of sorts. Don't be surprised if your friends and colleagues rally around you and feed off your vibe and good chemistry.

Sign #2: They enter, leave and reenter your life at various points

You are together, and then you are not, and then you are again. Despite the fact that you love each other more than anything, one of you (known as the "runner") seems to not be able to handle it, and the relationship dissolves. It's almost as though your connection is too intense for you to be consistently together for any extended period of time.

This is actually rather common among twin flames. They meet for a given period of time and then go their separate ways. Often, this is due to the need of improving upon themselves. That way, the next time they meet, they will be ready for one another. If not, they will leave each other and then resolve to come back together at some other point in time.

Sign #3: Your twin flame has expanded your mind in ways you may not have thought possible

With them, you exchange ideas, beliefs, religion, and so on. You've "awakened" because of their love. There is consistent jousting. Since they are your equal in many ways, they won't be afraid to challenge you or call you out. But don't take this the wrong way. They only mean it because they want to get the very best out of you.

Don't be surprised if they come to challenge your ideas and beliefs. They are not meant to be your "yes" man. They are meant to challenge you down to the very core of your being. They won't settle until they get the wheels turning inside your head and inside your heart. While they won't be challenging you to go astray, they will lead you to rethink virtually everything you have taken to be true in life.

Sign #4: You are the perfect complement to each other

They seem just like your other half, the parts of you that were missing all along. What you have yet to realize is that they are the parts of you, you have yet to know. Thus, they will help expand your perspective on your journey of self-discovery. They will help you put many more aspects of yourself into focus, thereby providing you with the opportunity to become a much stronger version of each other.

Bear in mind that this isn't about completing each other's sentences and liking the same foods. This is about filling in those gaps which you know, or may not know are there. They will hold the answers to those dark or incomplete parts of yourself. So, don't be surprised if they come to you with just the right answer at the right time.

Sign #5: You are so comfortable together

Upon meeting them, you immediately sense that you've known this person before. Your connection is too intense for you to have just been strangers – there is a deep feeling of familiarity when you're with them.

Indeed, it is like you have known them forever. The familiarity is so striking that you cannot put your finger on it. Yet, you will waste no time in becoming comfortable with one another. Whether it is a romantic or professional relationship, you will be in synch virtually from the get-go.

Sign #6: The period time in which your twin flame emerged is always marked by drastic change

They bring about a lot of intense transformation in your life, sometimes painfully so.

Regardless of the type of relationship, your twin flame will always usher in a new type of experience in your life. They will lead a transformational effect to such an extent that there will be a "before" and "after" you. This is how powerful this relationship can be. So, don't be surprised if your world is literally turned upside down when you meet them.

Please remember that they are here to test you and push you. So, the challenge they bring will change you in ways that you may not have thought possible. But when they do, you will never be able to go back. You will never be the same again.

Sign #7: Your connection is virtually immediate. So, your relationship progresses very quickly

Right off the bat, you "click" as though you've known each other forever. This only grows over time, and the more you get to know about them, the more absolutely in love you are.

In a romantic relationship, your affair moves so quickly that there is no hesitation you are a couple. You won't even have to formally acknowledge your relationship. It is simply understood that you are together and that is that.

In other types of relationships, your instant connection allows you to move forward at a very rapid pace. For instance, if you are business partners, this connection will enable you to advance your projects very quickly. In fact, it may even seem like you had everything done all along. The results you will produce will certainly be astounding especially to outside observers.

Sign #8: Your emotions are intuitive and almost irrational

These are the feelings and energies that have been in suppression, which they are there in part to help you recognize and heal.

As much as you try to reason why you feel the way you do, you just won't be able to. Your relationship is what it is, and you know it at gut level. You automatically know where this is going.

The floodgates may open to deeper personal and spiritual growth. So, you won't have to hesitate. Rather, you can just go with it. You will be able to ride that rush of energy into a deeper and more meaningful understanding of yourself and the universe around you.

Sign #9: Though your love and passion may be great, it will also be accompanied by an equal share of uncertainty

You may find yourself questioning a lot, asking yourself whether or not this is really love, or really what you want for your life. This is why you need to be ready emotionally as the rollercoaster ride may prove to be too much for you.

Other times, the relationship progresses so quickly that it may set out alarm bells in one, or both, partners. This leads to a lot of second guessing about the relationship. Naturally, this would be the case in a romantic relationship.

In other types of twin flame relationships, you may find a similar degree of uncertainty insofar as determining whether this person is for real. Given that your connection is so strong, you may lead to question your actions based on logic. So, this underscores the need for a deeper and more meaningful understanding of your higher self.

Sign #10: You are not just lovers

You are each other's teachers, best friends, therapists, and so on. You have such a deep and layered connection that you do a lot more for each other than just be romantic.

This is the epitome of a romantic relationship. You will not be content with an emotional, sexual and social relationship. You are equal in virtually every way. Also, you fill in the gaps where needed. Yet, your twin flame will push you to become more than you could have ever imagined.

Picture your twin flame pushing you to run that extra mile, to get your college degree, to start your own business or to take that trip you have been putting off for years.

Indeed, you are not just limited to the textbook definition of lovers. You are everything rolled up into one package. When you enter a relationship such as this, be ready because it is a rollercoaster filled with intense and memorable experiences.

Sign 11: It seems like you have this profound connection that must be destined, but you come into each other's life at the wrong time, or something else stands in the way of you being together

This is not a product of ill fate, rather, it is a sign that you're not meant to be together in the way you think you should. (The right thing at the wrong time is the wrong thing.)

When this happens, it might seem like a Greek tragedy. Whether lovers, or any other type of twin flame relationship, the fact that it is not the right time for you may signal that you need to be ready for the next time you two meet again. Perhaps the experience can help you see where you went wrong and what you need to go to improve for the next go-around.

Don't be surprised if you remain very close though not as close as you'd hope. Please bear in mind that these relationships transcend any physical boundary. So, even if you are not physically present, you are still spiritually connected.

Sign #12: You are always drawn back to them one way or another

It might seem inexplicable, but there is always something that draws you two together. It might be one of those "on-off" relationships. Or, it could be that you are not geographically close and may only see each other every so often.

Whatever the case, you will always have something that will draw the two of you close together. You won't have to find any excuses or any justifications; you will just manage to find the way to be together once and for all.

Sign #13: The road is often bumpy

This is because your twin flame serves to show you everything that needs to be healed within you. This is not to be confused with "love" being painful. Love is not painful. Everything that stands in the way can be, though.

So, please bear in mind that the road may be filled with all kinds of setbacks along the way. Nevertheless, the act of loving your twin flame will never be the issue. What may become an issue at some point is the circumstances that are surrounding you.

Therefore, don't be afraid to face things head on. The worst thing you could do is bail out on your twin flame when they need you the most. You can always face things together. After all, both of you, united, will be much stronger than anything else that comes your way.

Sign #14: You are totally in synch

It is almost telepathic. You can feel what they're feeling or know what they're thinking. It's as though you are one.

Throughout this book, we have described how your relationship is spiritual and transcends anything in the physical domain. So, you won't need a good data plan; the data is already built in! This is why it is so important for you to be attuned to your higher self. As you become closer to your higher selves, you won't need to pick up the phone to communicate. You just know exactly what is going on, in real time.

Sign #15: One is more "spiritual" while the other is more "practical"

One is more soulful, the other more practical. You teach each other the virtues of how you think and behave – that is part of your purpose. This is all part of the balancing act that both of you are putting together. You are not here to see if things work out. You are here to provide each with the companionship and support that you need in order to grow and develop into the person you need to be.

So, don't be surprised if in addition to being perfectly in synch, you are each other's ideal complement. So, if there is something that you cannot handle, the other will be there to pick up the slack and vice versa. Ultimately, you won't have a better partner than your twin flame!

Sign #16: While you may be completely different individuals, the similarities between you are striking

Maybe you were born on their favorite brother's birthday, or you met on a very significant weekend. Maybe you both went to the same type of elementary and high school, or you had the same college major. One or two of these things could just be coincidence, but with a twin flame, you'll probably have many overlapping similarities.

As such, there is always some type of uncommon, or unusual, coincidence that confirms you are meant to be together. Other times, you meet under the strangest of circumstances. These are twists of fate that not even the most talented writers could come up with. This is a definite sign that you were meant to be together in this lifetime.

Sign #17: They feel like family

This is your soul recognizing someone it's known before, or someone it's very close to. A telltale sign of this is meeting a complete stranger and just recognizing them immediately. No, this isn't a case of mistaken identity. This is a case of seeing someone and just knowing who they are.

Most people say that they immediately knew that this was their twin flame. Perhaps they couldn't rationalize it right there and then, but they instinctively knew this was the partner they had been looking for.

This sense of familiarity is so strong that most people will think you have known each other forever. You might even have similar physical characteristics. For instance, you might be the same height, or the same shoe size. There will be so many things about you that just fit well together.

Sign #18: They show you what you most desire as well as what you most fear

Their purpose is not (and has never been) to make you feel "settled" or comfortable, but to help introduce you to yourself. As such, this is the kind of relationship that will take you out of your comfort zone. If you believe that your twin flame is meant to "baby" you, you have another thing coming.

Your twin flame is all about pushing the envelope; making you test your boundaries time and time again. When you find your twin flame, they will be more demanding than you could ever have imagined. Yet, they will also prove to be everything you had ever wanted in another human being. As such, you won't be afraid to have them push you time and time again. You will love them and appreciate them for doing so.

How can you be sure they are the one?

You will never be able to rationalize the fact that they are the one. There is no scientific way in proving that they are the one you have been looking for. It would be great if there was a pill you could take. Or some type of machine which could detect it.

This is why the previous sections in this book have been devoted to getting you to become in synch with your higher self. That way, you will be able to automatically recognize who they are when you find them. While it may not necessarily be something that happens instantly, you will be able to recognize the signs.

In the event that you already know your twin flame, you will begin to recognize the signs. When you do, you will be able to understand why they are so important to you. Perhaps you have always felt they were important to you but never fully realized it. But when you finally see that they have been there all along, it will be like discovering a winning lottery ticket in your wallet. It is like finding hidden treasure in your back yard. It was there all along. But it wasn't until you decided to dig up some weeds and start a new garden that you realized the treasure had been there all along.

Chapter 14: The next steps after meeting your twin flame

"Have you ever felt really close to someone? So close that you can't understand why you and the other person have two separate bodies, two separate skins?"

-- Nancy Garden

Most stories and books out there focus on getting to the all-important twin flame encounter. Yet, they don't prepare you for what will happen after you meet them. No one ever really talks about the way in which you, and your life, will be different after meeting your twin flame.

Indeed, your life will never be the same. Your life will undergo a profound change that may, or may not, cause you to simply become a different person.

Nevertheless, one thing is for sure: anything you are going through will pop up at this point. So, if you are working on or dealing with any issues, they will come up during this time. You will also feel compelled to get away from certain people or certain circumstances.

That is why a twin flame encounter usually marks the beginning of a change cycle in which you will have to make some important choices. Therefore, this chapter is devoted to discussing 11 changes that you may go through in the aftermath of meeting your twin flame.

Of course, these changes affect different folks to a varying degree, your ability to recognize these potential shifts in your life will allow you to make sense of what you need to do in order to gain your ascension.

One of the most important reasons for this life-changing effect that the twin flame encounter has on us, is the fact that it puts us on the fast track to ascension. This ties in closely to the twin flame mission, because as twin flames we have come in this time, dimension and reality to assist in the ascension of one another in addition to helping others find their own way. Now, this might seem overwhelming to you, but please bear in mind that your twin flame will not only help you help yourself, but they will also help you help others.

At this moment, the ascension process is all about helping both of you reach a higher level of consciousness and awareness, thereby connecting you with the universe and everything around it. It might sound a bit too much for now. It might sound like you have this enormous task ahead. However, the journey for finding yourself will lead you to also discover the universe. This is why your twin flame is meant to walk with you along the way and not just nudge you in the direction that you need to go.

While everyone is on the same path, with some moving faster than others, the fact of the matter is that having your twin flame beside you is a way of fast tracking the process. You will have a boost that, unfortunately, many others may not get. It is true that we all get the same chance, but not everyone is ready to take advantage of it.

Given the fact that meeting your twin flame is all about helping you shift into a higher level of consciousness, you will find that some of these changes will have such a profound impact on you that you will begin to question many things about your life. This can lead to a fundamental paradigm shift in your life. In essence, you are doing away with the old and ushering in the new.

This shifting out of this old paradigm and shifting into this new perception of reality is what turns your world so upside down after you have met your twin flame. It is also the cause of many of the seemingly unrelated changes you go through after meeting your twin here on Earth. So, in fact they are side effects due to your paradigm shift. While they are not immediate, that is, they won't be happening within 15 minutes of meeting your twin flame, they will be well on their way. Then, when the process of ascension takes hold of you, you will begin to notice how the changes in your life begin to take shape.

As such, it is important for you to recognize them and embrace them in the best possible way. If you suddenly find yourself resisting change, then you might end up interrupting the process, or simply making it harder than it has to be.

So, let's look at some of the side effects that this paradigm shift brings with it and that as a twin flame you most likely will be experiencing, without understanding that it is all a part of the process you are in. Bringing in this understanding will help you feel more focused and take things more seriously, as you start to see that others are going through the same process as you are. What this means is that you will find others, other sets of twin flame, who are going through the same process as you are.

In any event, keep an eye for these changes. They may start out subtly but make no mistake: they will approach you in a hurry. And once they are upon you, you can use them to turbo charge your ascension process... alongside your twin flame.

Shift #1: Some friends may go, and new friends may come

When you shift out of your old paradigm perception of reality you will find that this creates a disconnect with many of the people you considered friends before. You will no longer be the same and they will notice this. In a way, it is like you are on a new wavelength now. On top of this your raised vibrational frequency can also make former friends and buddies feel uncomfortable around you because you are no longer a vibrational match.

As a twin flame, you may also experience that hardly anyone in your circle of friends really understands the process you are in. Given that most of the people around you may not be in the same situation as you, that is, going through their own twin flame journey, then your sudden attachment to your new flame (literally) may seem odd and perhaps too much to handle.

No matter how much you try, you can't make your friends understand that your twin is the first person in your life that has seen your true self and still loves you. This is because the only frame of reference your friends have for romantic love is the old paradigm template of fear-based love common in traditional society. This template is incompatible with the twin flame connection because the twin flame dynamic is all about loving each other no matter what.

All of these factors will move people out of your life, some that you may have known since childhood – because they just don't get you anymore. But the main reason is due to the fact that you don't match their frequency anymore.

One of the side effects that comes with this shift in paradigm and vibration is that you will begin to meet other like-minded individuals. So, you will basically change one set of friends for another. Of course, this doesn't mean that you are going to be cutting people out of your life on purpose. Just don't be surprised to find that you will be associating with a different crowd.

Shift #2: A possible career shift

The paradigm shift that may come within your mindset may lead you to seek another line of work or employment. The point here is to find something which better resonates with the way you feel inside. You may find that your current job, or even career, just doesn't seem like a good fit for you anymore. You might even be fired from your job or go bankrupt in your old company. Your soul will do whatever it takes to help you shift to the new timeline that you are meant to be on.

This calls for trust and surrender in order to move through the apparent appearance of loss, while you are being shifted into the life your soul has prepared for you. This process might be uncomfortable as ever to go through, but it will definitely force you outside of your comfort zone. This is especially true if your new line of work – your soul calling, turns out to be a considerable change as compared to what you are currently doing.

The trick is to understand that this is shift. It is a way that you are transitioning from your old paradigm to your new paradigm based on the ascension process triggered by your twin flame.

Shift #3: Time spent with family will change

This disconnect with your friends may also extend to your family. This may cause you to drastically limit your time with certain family members. If you come from a toxic family dynamic, you might actually decide to break with some family members for good.

This does not have to conflict with forgiveness. You can forgive someone completely in your heart and yet still not want to spend any time with them in the here and now. Forgiving someone does not equal to having to continue a relationship with that person. It often opens the possibility of continuing the relationship but you don't have to. If someone remains toxic in their behavior, you can still forgive them for your sake and your own health, but there is nothing that says that you must continue spending time with them.

Family often comes with a lot of drama. As you shift into a higher frequency, you will develop zero tolerance for all of this unnecessary drama that only keeps you from what you really came to accomplish in this lifetime. When you start looking at life from your twin flame's perspective, all this family drama becomes pointless – it may not be worth getting upset over or wasting your energy on.

It might also occur that family members will leave your life voluntarily, most likely blaming you for the disconnect they feel. When this happens, it might be the result of clashing vibrations among family members. So, it is best not to take it personally.

Just because you were born into the same family or this person gave birth to you, it does not obligate you to stick with this person unconditionally. Sometimes, staying away is the most loving response you can give to a family member.

Shift #4: Developing a "zero tolerance"

Ascending into a higher frequency might lead you to develop a lack of tolerance for some of the following attitudes and circumstances:

Intimidation

Bullying

Cheating (both romantically and professionally)

Lying

Gossiping

Hypocrisy

Backstabbing

Many of these attitudes may be present in your place of work. This is why you may end up changing jobs or careers. Many of these attitudes can lead to a toxic environment. So, needless to say, this is hardly conducive to your personal ascension.

Shift #5: You might even end up moving house... or city

As everything in this world is literally made of energy, including the things that seem immovable in nature such as a house and furniture – the shift into a new paradigm will also affect these expressions of energy in your life.

If your current living arrangements are not aligned to the higher frequency which you are shifting into, you will most likely move house as well. This may happen very abruptly or very fluently depending on whatever experience best suits your soul evolution.

Some twin flames become homeless, others drift abroad for years – but the shift does not have to be this dramatic. The transition could also come very easily and effortlessly. No matter how you get there, the shift will eventually move you into a living arrangement that best supports you and your mission for this lifetime.

Shift #6: Your body will also begin to look differently

Your body will also see some of the effects of your twin flame encounter. If you have been going through a rough patch, you might find that the change in your mindset will lead your body to begin healing itself.

In addition, you may find the following changes in your diet:

Junk food isn't as tasty as it used to be

You may consume less sugar and caffeine

You might consider becoming vegan or vegetarian

Alcohol and recreational drugs may not appeal to you

You will consider cutting out unhealthy foods all together

The food and drink you consume will be more in line, more in synch with your new vibration and paradigm shift. So, do pay attention to what your body is asking you for.

Shift #7: A twin flame romance may lead you to lose interest in ordinary relationships

In the case of romantic relationships, the depth of connection among the two halves may leave such a lasting impact that ordinary romantic relationships pale in comparison.

What this means is that it is very common for twin flames to decide to abstain from relationships until they can be with their twin or someone else with whom they have a similar profound connection. This also means waiting until they can experience deep love with another person on a similar vibrational level.

As such, you might feel that engaging in a romantic relationship with someone who is not on the same wavelength as you is not worth it. You are "saving yourself," in a manner of speaking, for someone with whom you can truly connect on a deeper level.

Sign #8: Alcohol and drugs go by the wayside

Raising your personal vibrational frequency also has an effect on your tolerance for toxins. This includes more subtle things such as sugar or caffeine, to harder substances such as alcohol, nicotine or drugs.

Part of the issue is that your system will be less tolerant to these substances. For instance, you hit your maximum tolerance level much sooner even on lower levels of such substances. In general, as you raise your vibrational frequency you become more sensitive, to sounds, light, other people's vibrations, chemicals, perfumes, make-up, certain foods, and so on.

But because raising your vibrational frequency also makes you more committed to living in the here and now, many twin flames who were addicted to alcohol and drugs found themselves no longer needing alcohol or drugs to drown out reality. Instead, they cleaned up their life thereby leaving their addictions behind them.

If your twin flame is currently on drugs or abusing alcohol, please bear in mind that this is part of their personal journey. You cannot "help" someone beat addiction. The best way to help them is to keep working on raising your own vibrational frequency. If they are your true twin flame this will have a clear effect on them.

Shift #9: Sexual relationships will never be the same

In romantic relationships, sexual encounters undergo a tremendous shift. This is due to the deep and spiritual connection between the two flames. If you found yourself engaging in superficial or casual encounters in the past, then you might feel that going back to such relationships may not satisfy you anymore.

Since you have made a deep connection with the other half of your soul, nothing else can compare to that. You will find that attempting to connect with another person in the same manner may not be quite as easy.

As such, you will begin to abstain from engaging in relationships with other people with whom you don't feel a similar connection. This deeper connection transcends any kind of physical attraction. Though physical attraction is certainly important, a lack of a spiritual and emotional connection may lead you to refrain from engaging in relationships with some people

Shift #10: You will begin to share your spiritual gifts

It almost becomes second-nature to begin sharing your newfound consciousness and understanding of the world with others around you.

This is why many twin flames get into fields like teaching after their twin flame encounters. These are folks who had high-paying jobs and then suddenly left a big bank or Wall Street firm to help poor people in Africa.

Those who are not on the same wavelength may never be able to understand such decisions. When you are attuned to your higher self during this process of ascension, then you will not hesitate to use your spiritual gift for the benefit of others.

Your twin flame will more than likely join you on this path. They will support you in the same mission even if it is in a different capacity. For example, you might find your twin flame supporting your mission in Africa, though they might be working in health care while you work in education. While the roles are different, the mission is the same.

Shift #11: You are no longer ego-driven

Now, this isn't to say that you were selfish or egotistic in the past. This is meant to say that your ego will no longer factor in, in any of the decisions your make, or the attitude you put forth. Your ego will take a step back to the ultimate purpose outlined by your higher self.

When you fail to put yourself ahead of others, you will begin to notice how everything tends to have a much deeper and more spiritual meaning. So, you are not concerned about how something affects you, rather, you are concerned about how things affect others.

This is a direct result of the shift in your mindset and your paradigm. Again, this will lead many individuals to leave profitable and lucrative careers to focus on ones which help others. While you are not required to do this, you may feel compelled to do so.

One happy medium is to engage in volunteer work. So, you may not leave your current career. But you can balance out your feelings and desire to help by engaging in charity work. Some individuals become anonymous donors or support causes without seeking adulation and publicity. They just do it because they want to.

Chapter 15: The 8 stages of a twin flame relationship

"Love is like a friendship caught on fire. In the beginning a flame, very pretty, often hot and fierce, but still only light and flickering. As love grows older, our hearts mature and our love becomes as coals, deep-burning and unquenchable."

-- Bruce Lee

In this chapter, we will be taking a deeper look at how a twin flame relationship dynamic plays out. The stages described herein are more in line with a romantic relationship though their core principles can apply to a friendship, professional collaboration or even a family relationship. Whatever the case, you will find that many of these traits play out to varying degrees.

So, it is important that once you have started down the path of the twin flame journey, you are mentally and emotionally ready to make the most of this journey. Your self-discovery will lead you to become one with your higher self. By extension, you will also be pushing your twin flame to do their part in order to earn their ascension as well.

As such, we will describe eight stages. You may hear and read about 10 or even 15 stages. While the number of stages, as such, may vary according to different opinions, the transition process tends to be the same. So, let's get started by taking a deeper look at this dynamic.

Stage #1: "The one"

We have been ingrained from childhood that there is one person out there that will find us and make us happy. But you have endured chaotic, unreliable, and challenging loves in your life. You believe that the stories you've heard are fictional and disappointing. The moment you meet your twin flame, that entire mentality and belief system disappears. You begin to understand and accept that "the one" has been searching for you as intensely as you have them. You cannot believe that this is real. But you give in to the possibility. And if you do, this person helps you regain a love for life that you believed could never exist.

One word of caution: meeting "the one" is often romanticized by popular culture. Books and movies portray this pent-up emotion that explodes in a crescendo of love and fulfillment. While a twin flame relationship certainly feels that way, "the one" may not come into your life in such a dramatic fashion. If anything, they may discreetly enter your life. It is up to you to discover when that moment takes place. Consequently, it is certainly worth taking this into consideration. Otherwise you might find yourself disappointed that "the one" did not enter your life in a horse-drawn carriage.

Stage #2: You understand why they are here

When you start to accept that this person has undergone similar experiences, it becomes clear that you had to reach this point in your life to accept this kind of relationship. Twin flames enter our lives at the precise moment that we require to learn something incredible about ourselves. Many times, a twin flame comes into your life when you are in another committed relationship. You may be married, engaged, or dealing with the loss of your mate. This person shows up with incredible wisdom that you need to hear in order to move on. And, it is then that you also realize that if this person had come into your life earlier, you would have taken the experience for granted.

Given your immediate connection, you won't want to waste any time in getting your relationship off the ground. Yet, there is still an adjustment period as you might be coming from completely different walks of life. While you might feel tempted to give your entire life the heave-ho, it is always best to proceed with caution. Often, rushing into a twin flame relationship may end up causing more harm than good. So, take the time to consider what it would take for the both of you to come together. Perhaps the most obvious arrangement may not be the best for either of you. Thus, you may have to explore alternative relationship arrangements.

Stage #3: Then, there is love...

There is a difference between loving someone and truly falling in love with them. We love our parents, our friends, family members, and other past lovers. When you meet your twin flame, those forms of love cannot measure up to the intensity and passion of your other half. You do not have to force the love, or try to make sense of it. For the first time, your heart knows something that your mind cannot analytically put together. Falling in love is the easiest thing in the world. It becomes the most natural substance of the union. Twin flames aren't blinded by reality, because they are their own world. Illusions fall short of this fire. This is the phase of pure ecstasy because you allow the heart to do what it is there to do: love unconditionally.

While this is mainly skewed toward a romantic relationship, you can develop profound love for your twin flame in a non-romantic relationship. The same unconditional acceptance and support is there. You will not hesitate to be the helping hand your friend needs every time. So, developing love does not necessarily imply a romantic relationship every time.

Stage #4: You begin to learn so much about yourself

Every relationship teaches something valuable about the self. Once the initial passion starts to stabilize and daily routine takes over, you begin to witness the many aspects of yourself. Twin flames not only have the same magical and wonderful dispositions, but they also mirror the dark parts of our souls. It's in this space that we must learn to heal, forgive and partake in accepting all aspects of the self. It is always easy to live in the light of all goodness, but we are made in duality: dark vs. light, good vs. bad, and so on. These are the moments that we must be mature to understand that there is always soul work to be done in this human experience. This person will heighten all facets of ourselves.

While false flames may provide you with the jolt you need to wake up and get moving, your twin flame will hold your hand through many of the self-discovery tasks you need to go through. If you have come a long way on your own, then you may not have that much to deal with.

On the flip side, you may be the one who has to lead your twin flame into a deeper and more profound understanding of themselves. Please bear in mind that you are not there to give answers. Rather, the twin flame dynamic is about helping each other find the way to the right answers. This is a huge difference.

As such, a false flame may give you with a cheat sheet with all of the answers to the test. Your twin flame will show you to get to the answer. So, they won't help you cheat for the test; they will help you study for it. This is a huge difference.

Stage #5: You might become a flight risk

The depth and dimension of this love affair is sometimes too much for someone to handle. You recognize parts of yourself that you aren't willing to look at. In those moments, you start to put on your running shoes. The first few stages of twin flame relationships often times look like the coyote and roadrunner. You can't help but chase after each other in circles. It's in these times that you get to witness all the similarities in each other. Fear and anxiety become the judging mates for egotistical decisions. Are you willing to continue?

Throughout this book, we mentioned the "runner and chaser" dynamic. Since a twin flame relationship is the real deal, some folks may not be ready for such an incredible rush of emotions. So, they may become a flight risk, that is, they may push away from the table. They may feel overwhelmed and decide they need space.

When this happens, then the runner begins going after the chaser. Hence, the coyote and roadrunner metaphor is truly appropriate. This dynamic might become magnified is the chaser has attachment issues that are triggered by the runner. So, it may end up damaging the twin flame relationship even to a point beyond repair.

The most important thing to keep in mind is that if this dynamic develops, one needs to stop running and the other needs to stop chasing. In a way, it is like looking for something you have lost. You find it once you have stopped looking for it.

Thus, the runner needs space to get a grip on their feelings while the chaser needs to stop chasing and take a breather. At the end of the day, both flames will come back to each other. However, if the relationship has been damaged, they may need some time apart before they can become successful together.

In the meantime, it is a great opportunity to determine what went wrong. The soul searching that ensues a failed attempt at a twin flame relationship can reveal so much about you. So, take a possible failure as a lesson rather than a tragedy. Your twin flame will always be there. But you might just have to be patient about it.

Stage #6: You give in

All that running away and running around gets exhausting. You wear each other out. It's in this stage that you know that this is going to take some adjusting. You and your twin flame are willing to enter this experiment of cosmic challenges. You recognize that there is work to be done, and together you can accomplish it. Once you set ego aside, you feel the love and fear dissolves. This is when you start to understand the soul contract that was created many lifetimes ago. This is the phase when you both can find peace in the union.

At this point, both of you have decided to quit running around in circles.

Now, please bear in mind that giving in is about surrendering to one another. It is not about foregoing who you are or what you believe in. It is not about giving up control over to the other flame. This is about making the conscious decision that you are meant to be together and now is the time.

Of course, if you are faced with adverse circumstances, then it might not be so simple. Nevertheless, you have decided that the time to go on the journey, as a whole, has come. The end result is a relationship based on mutual trust and collaboration.

Ultimately, you will not second-guess your decision. Rather, you will feel satisfied that you made the right choice at the best time.

Stage #7: You push each other

The moment you surrender without fear of this person taking off, the easier it is to settle into a healthy relationship. Twin flames have the strongest ability of making each other succeed. They are each other's cheerleaders, coaches, and audience. Your twin will pull and push you with love and encouragement beyond any other relationship in your life. They will not stand in your way while you follow your purpose. Sometimes twin flames separate for just a bit during this transition as they find grounding in their own lives. But, out of mutual love and respect, they return with power and ambition to run side by side on this journey of life.

By this stage, you have already settled into your dynamic. You are now consistently pushing each other to become the best you could possibly become. You are not looking to waste any time on useless tasks. You are looking to become masters of your fate. As such, you are not concerned with less meaningful tasks. This is all about developing your personal skills for your personal mission.

This is where both of your goals and plans come to fruition. Even if you happen to dabble in completely different careers and jobs, the task is still the same. The mission will not change. You are still on the same journey. You are still looking to fulfill the same person.

Consequently, you are after producing the same results. You are not concerned about who is first or who is the best. In fact, you may find yourselves taking turns in the spotlight. If one has a tremendous success one day, the other will follow that up the next.

Since your ego is no longer in the driver's seat, you will have no trouble dealing with your partner's success. In fact, your relationship will lead to collaboration in such a way that it doesn't matter who gets credit. The only thing that matters is that you got the job done.

Stage #8: Wholeness

Once the ego is no longer dictating the partnership, the heart mends and becomes one. You and your twin flame become a powerhouse of love, empathy and compassion for each other. And this is contagious for everyone around you. You are the epitome of true unconditional love. Fear is no longer a valuable commodity. You have both worked through heartache. The mirror lives from past experiences have served as a union for this exact moment when you accept this type of love. Twin flames recognize each other's vibration and frequency. They become one in rhythm. The oneness of their coupling isn't only through the death of egotistical beliefs. It's in the process of letting go that the heart recognizes why you need each other. You are here to make a difference in your lives.

One of the most misunderstood results of the twin flame dynamic is that both individuals surrender their individuality for the sake of the union.

If you find yourself giving up your individuality for the other, then that is not a true twin flame relationship. A true twin flame will support you in developing who you are. You don't have to give up anything for the sake of your twin flame. Your flame will be there to support you in becoming what you have set out to be.

As such, we are not talking about wearing the same clothes or speaking in unison. We are talking about complementing each other perfectly. So, even if you have different tastes and different opinions on things, you respect each other's individuality. Ultimately, you are on the same team. It just might be that you are playing different positions.

A true twin flame relationship will always bolster your personal identity. After all, they are looking to help you develop yourself. And that will never be at the expense of who you truly are.

On the flip side, if you find yourself attempting to impose your will on your twin flame, then you might run the risk of damaging your relationship. There is no need for you to impose your will on anybody. All you have to do to make sure that you are on the same page. If you do happen to run into differences, don't worry, it happens all the time. The main thing is to let love and understanding lead the way when you don't happen to see eye to eye on something.

The final word

In this book, we have had an extensive discussion on the twin flame dynamic and relationship. If you have already found "the one," then congratulations. You have already done something momentous.

If you are still looking for "the one," don't fret. They will come along soon enough. In the meantime, you need to take this opportunity to improve upon yourself and what you need to do in order to be ready for your twin flame. If you happen to find that you are becoming desperate, then you need to take a step back.

Often, we lose sight of what is in front of us because we become obsessed with an idea. When you become obsessed with anything in life, it becomes hard to see the forest for the trees. As such, try your best to keep your eyes on the prize: self-development and fulfillment.

You already have everything you need in order to become the one that your twin flame needs. So now, it is just a matter of polishing up who you are. That way, when the time comes, you will truly build a solid relationship based on trust, mutual understanding and collaboration.

There is simply not much more you can ask for in life.

Conclusion

"My body's been touched a thousand or more times, but I am craving something so much deeper than that - I desire to be felt, right down to the core of my soul and the corners of my heart. That's what love is about, isn't it - cracking yourself open to the possibility that it could change your life."

-- Nikki Rowe

Wow! It seems like we only started this journey a few moments ago and look where we are now.

We discussed a great deal of things in this book. Please take the time to go back to any sections which you feel you may need to review.

We have gone over a good number of lists and signs. Definitely, it can be a lot to take in. Nevertheless, we have covered virtually everything you could possibly need in order to be ready for your twin flame.

By now, if you are sure you have met your twin flame, then kudos to you. You have achieved something amazing in life that few people have actually managed to find.

If you are still thinking, wondering, if that magical someone is out there, rest assured that they are. If they are not by your side at the moment, then take it as an opportunity to improve upon yourself. That way, when the time comes to meet, you will be more than ready for them.

Being ready transcends a physical dimension. Sure, you might be compelled to lose weight, get in shape and just feel better about yourself physically. But it also entails a spiritual dimension which may not be easy for you to deal with right away.

The healing process of all your emotional blockages and the baggage from the past is a requisite. You cannot expect to save a successful twin flame relationship if you plan to dump all your issues on your twin flame. While not being "ready" does not preclude your encounter, it will just make your twin flame relationship that much harder to succeed at.

As such, there are three final points to consider before engaging in your twin flame relationship.

Consideration #1: You will never stop growing, learning and improving.

Your journey to self-development and improvement will never end. You cannot expect to graduate one day from improving upon yourself. It just doesn't work that way. A twin flame relationship is about turbocharging your self-discovery and learning process. There are many things about yourself that you are yet to discover. And while you may have made considerable strides up to now, there is still a long way to go.

Unfortunately, we don't really know how deep our journey toward self-discovery and fulfillment really goes. In fact, this road is more like a rabbit hole. The deeper you go, the more you realize there is a lot left to go.

If you are still looking for your twin flame, take this opportunity to truly learn about yourself as much as you can. By the time you eventually meet your twin flame, you will have achieved an understanding of yourself that will give both of you a fighting chance. It is undoubted that taking the time to learn more about yourself is akin to an investment. The more money you put in, the more you can get out of it. Thus, the more time and effort that you put into, the more you will be able to get out of it.

As mentioned earlier, if you are looking to dump your baggage and your issues on your twin flame, then you might find yourself sorely disappointed. It might be that your twin flame may not be able to cope with their own baggage in addition to yours. This can be fuel for runner and chaser dynamic.

If you should happen to fall prey to this dynamic, restoring your relationship to a point of balance may require a great deal of work. As such, it will be up to both of you to decide if you are truly ready to take on such a complex task. Otherwise, you may need to part ways and heal on your own.

This is why you need to take advantage of every opportunity to improve upon yourself and the gifts you have to offer to your twin flame. The more you can improve yourself, the better off your twin flame will be.

Consideration #2: It's not about you, it's about your twin flame.

Earlier, we mentioned how the shift in your paradigm will take the focus away from your ego and place it on your twin flame. If you really think about it, focusing on your twin flame is like focusing on yourself. Whatever you do to help improve your twin flame will rub off on you in a very positive manner. Likewise, if you make life difficult for your twin flame, this will also rub off on you but in a negative manner.

Consequently, putting your twin flame ahead of yourself is one of the most important decisions that you can make on this journey. Of course, this isn't about giving yourself up completely for the sake of your twin flame. There is no one asking you to pay the ultimate price for your flame's happiness. The fact of the matter is that this should be a mutual purpose for both flames.

In the end, putting your flame ahead of yourself will provide you with a great feeling of satisfaction and fulfillment. You are giving yourself completely to your other half. There are no egos, nor are there any selfish thoughts. Please bear in mind that a false flame will lead you to believe that it is about you, and not about anyone else.

When you are in a false flame relationship, the journey of self-discovery and self-development is solely focused on one of the two partners. The reason for this is that false flames are not meant to be your unconditional partner on your journey. If anything, they fill a specific purpose. They have an important lesson that you must learn. Now, that lesson could be a very nice and pleasant one or it could be a harsh and difficult one. Whatever the lesson may be, a false flame will be focused on you. Therefore, you are the one who has to do most of the work. The learning and understanding that you extract from it, will help you grow as an individual. In fact, it may be an important step that you need to take in order to be ready for your true twin flame.

So, don't be surprised if your journey of self-discovery and self-improvement somehow meshes with that of your twin flame. Please keep in mind that you are both on the same journey; you are both on the same road. Of course, there may come a time when you need to part ways. This is something perfectly normal especially if you have fulfilled the purpose that you both had for each other in this lifetime.

When twin flames part ways, it is because they have fulfilled the role they had set out for each other in this lifetime. The next step on the road must be taken individually. When that happens, there are other lessons to be learned and other souls to be met. You may encounter additional false flames who hold the key to the next lessons which you must learn.

Think about it in these terms:

You have finished one grade at school, and therefore, you must move on to a new class with a new teacher. You may have new classmates and even an entirely new school. But the lessons which you must learn are equally important to your personal development. If you fail to learn them, you may find yourself falling behind in your personal development. But fear not, your flame will come back to you at some point down the road.

Consideration #3: A twin flame relationship is a work in progress.

Contrary to popular belief, a twin flame relationship is not "perfect." Yes, it does *feel* perfect, but it is still very much a work in progress. You cannot expect everything to be absolutely flawless. There will always be issues which you need to work on and improve.

As such, since twin flame relationships are a "work in progress" you need to strive to improve upon yourself and upon each other. When you work in tandem, you can help each other to improve your dynamic.

When you strive to improve your dynamic, then you will find that it won't be quite as hard as you think. While it might not be that hard to deal with, you still need to put in the time and effort needed to help the relationship grow.

If you believe that you can reach a point where everything is perfect, that may be a signal that you may need to part ways. When this happens, it could signal that there are lessons which you need to learn away from your twin flame.

This is the main reason why twin flames tend to come in and out of your life. There is nothing wrong with that. It just means that you cannot expect to be with them every minute of every day. It is certainly sad to part ways. However, it is generally a pre-requisite on the road to becoming whole.

When you are aware of the fact that your relationship is a work in progress, then you will find that you can put in the work that you need in order to develop your relationship as much as possible. This will foster the bond between you. But you can't expect everything to be a bed of roses.

In fact, conflict is where you can see if they are the real deal. A false flame will begin to fade away. On the other hand, a true twin flame will give you the love and support you need. In addition, the very nature of human existence makes it so that your relationship becomes a work in progress.

Please bear in mind that as a work in progress, you will always have room for improvement. If you happen to believe that there is a chance for everything to be perfect, then you need to take a long look at why you feel this way.

Nevertheless, you must strive to be perfect. Now, that doesn't mean that you should become obsessed with perfection. It is just a question of striving to make an effort to be the best you can possibly be. That is why being on the same page is so important to achieving harmony among twin flames.

Final considerations

At this point, you are ready for the next step in your personal journey. Please bear in mind that we are all on the same road. The main difference may lie at the point in which we find ourselves in. Some may be farther along than others. What this means is that you have to consider that your twin flame may be ahead of you, or behind you. While that is irrelevant to a certain extent, the point of meeting is just that: to help each other move farther along the path.

Given the fact that you are on this journey to self-discovery, it is often easy to confuse a soulmate for a twin flame. Likewise, it is also very common to confuse a false flame with a twin flame. If you should happen to become confused, you may believe that "the one" comes with a great deal of drama.

This is something to keep in mind:

"The one" does not come with drama. "The one" comes with all the bells and whistles. The drama may ensue as a result of the circumstances that you are living in. "The one" is all about peace and harmony. As such, you won't have to worry about them making your life overly complicated. If anything, your twin flame is all about making life easier for you to cope with.

Of course, they won't let you off the hook easily, that is, they will strive to help you become a better person. But that is just a side effect of the circumstances that come with having your twin flame in your life.

Nevertheless, keep in mind that having your twin flame is well worth the challenges that you may have to encounter. It is the type of experience that will mark you for the rest of your life.

At this time, all we have left to say is that the journey has now reached a new step. The journey has reached a new milestone.

This book has been another step in that journey. Whatever your twin flame dynamic, you will find that consistently working and improving upon yourself will make life that much better for you. Regardless of whether you are currently in the presence of your twin flame, working on improving yourself will never be a waste of time and effort. You will have the opportunity to improve the lives of those around. As such, you will have the chance to become a positive influence for those around you.

Please keep in mind that you have a mission to complete on this Earth during this timeline. You are the only one who can actually determine what that is. If you find yourself trying to live up to the expectations of others, or trying to please others around you, then you will be living the kind of life which will neither fulfill you nor bring you true happiness.

Everything you need to be happy, to become truly fulfilled, is residing inside of you.

If you have found this book to be interesting and informative, do leave a comment or review. There are many others, just like you, who are seeking to find a light on this path. They are seeking the same things which you are striving to find.

By leaving your comments, you will aid those who are looking to find their true twin flame. Please bear in mind that part of your higher self's mission on this Earth is to help others. Also, do not hesitate to share the information which you have learned in this book.

Just like you, there are others who may need a nudge in the right direction. You can provide that nudge. As such, you have the power in your hands to become a positive influence on the lives of those around you.

Made in United States
Troutdale, OR
03/07/2025